GOLAN LEVIN
LIA
META
ADRIAN WARD

GENERATIVE DESIGN: BEYOND PHOTOSHOP

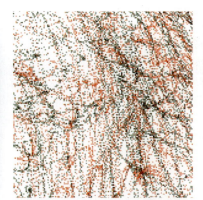

Trademark Acknowledgements

First printed December 2001

Published by friends of ED Ltd. 30 Lincoln Road, Olton, Birmingham. B27 6PA
Printed in India by Ajanta Offset & Packagings Ltd., New Delhi
ISBN 1903450470

GENERATIVE DESIGN: BEYOND PHOTOSHOP

credits

authors
golan levin
lia
meta
adrian ward

author agent
jez booker

project administrator
fionnuala meacher

copyright research
fionnuala meacher

index
simon collins
emily colborne

content architect
catherine o'flynn

lead editor
jim hannah

editor
julie closs

graphic editor
katy freer

technical reviewers
corné van dooren
andrés yánez durán
anne lacquoet
jeroen meeuwissen
todd simon
peter walker

technical consultants
peter aylward
kristian besley

creative consultant
sunny ralph
www.freshfroot.com

GOLAN LEVIN

Golan Levin is an artist, composer and designer interested in developing artifacts and experiences which explore supple new modes of audiovisual expression. His work has focused on the design of systems for the creation and performance of simultaneous image and sound, as part of a more general examination of communications protocols for individual engagement and non-verbal dialogue. Most recently, Levin presented Dialtones: A Telesymphony (2001), an audiovisual concert whose sounds are wholly performed through the carefully-choreographed ringing of the audience's own mobile phones. Levin was granted an Award of Distinction in the Prix Ars Electronica for his Audiovisual Environment Suite (2000) interactive software and its accompanying audiovisual performance, Scribble (2000). Levin received undergraduate and graduate degrees from the MIT Media Laboratory, where he studied with John Maeda in the Aesthetics and Computation Group. Prior to this, he worked as an interaction designer and research scientist at Interval Research Corporation for four years. He currently resides in New York City.

LIA

lia, "graphikprogrammer", based in vienna, working with computers since 1995.

websites:
www.silverserver.co.at/lia
www.re-move.org
www.turux.org
www.wofbot.org

META

meta is an individual living somewhere in the world.
meta is a work in progress.
meta's website can be found at http://meta.am/.
one day meta will be dead.
when that day comes, the words, sounds, and images that
meta produced
are all that will remain to prove that meta ever existed.
please save a backup copy.

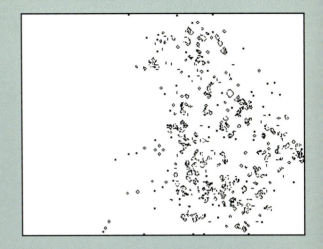

ADRIAN WARD

Adrian Ward works as a software artist, creating generative audio, visual and process-based applications for a variety of uses. He is mostly concerned with issues surrounding authorship and the extension of aesthetic subjectivity into code – an activity which he believes has been happening since the first programmable devices were invented.

Currently collaborating with a range of musicians, conceptual and performance artists, he also uses his software for live musical performances and installations. He is involved with a number of educational software projects that actively engage the user by exploring interactivity within a generative context.

Ade has had his work published by Lovebytes (Sheffield), MediaSpace (Plymouth) and Rhizome (New York), had software exhibited at 291 Gallery (London) and the New Museum of Contemporary Art (NYC), and has presented papers at two International Generative Art conferences (Milan) as well as giving a guest lecture at Cornish College of the Arts (Seattle). His most ambitious project to date – Auto-Illustrator, a generative vector graphic design application – co-won the Transmediale.01 Artistic Software award (Berlin) and earned an honorary mention at the 2001 Prix Ars Electronica (Linz) in the Interactive Art category.

"I'd like to thank Alex McLean for encouraging me to think about code in the way that I do. I pinched his computer-as-stone metaphor. His original paper is at http://www.generative.net/papers/hacking. I'd also like to thank Geoff Cox and everyone else at STAR in Plymouth for educating me and giving me interesting things to do with code. And I'd also like to thank everyone involved in this book – the people at friends of ED, and the other authors, who I deeply admire for the astounding attitudes they possess with regards to their work, and code in general. There is an endless list of other people I want to thank too for their inspiration – too many to list here unfortunately. Watch the scrolling credits in Auto-Illustrator for a (hopefully) complete list."

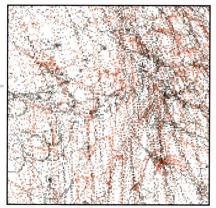

LIA: 7

ADRIAN WARD: 65

META: 105

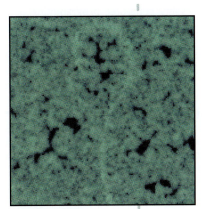

GOLAN: 159

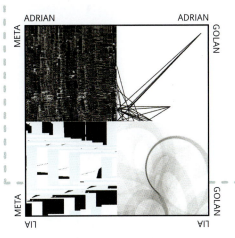

NOISE AND INTERFERENCE 225

The 4

Most of us program: whether it's setting our VCRs to record at certain times, or heating up our ready meals in a microwave. For most though, this confidence seems to fall far short of tackling a line of code.

The 4x4 authors seek to demystify computer programming and coding. They see no rupture between our everyday engagement with machines and technology, and the creation of tools to generate visual patterns.

This book aims to empower and has one message: control the means of production and shape your own creativity.

The 4x4

This book is a laboratory where you can learn from and participate in experimentation.

The 4x4 Project is a catalyst, and the authors' words, the readers' thoughts, the artworks and the theories are all ongoing reactions in the creative process. The book places you at the heart of the creative process, alongside the authors as they work to create their original commissioned pieces, and it pushes you off in new directions to create your own unique visions. No one is a spectator in the dynamic 4x4 environment.

The accompanying web site provides you with relevant source files for the tutorials, the final generative pieces, and all remixes and digital hybrids spawned by the Project... the next step is yours.

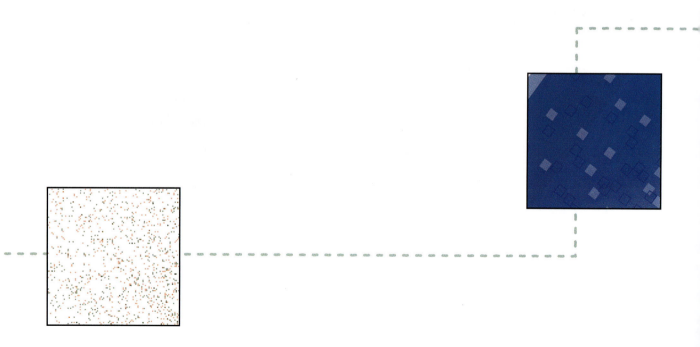

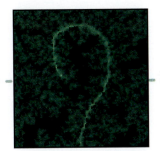

enter the 4x4 project

phase 1 - the book in your hand
phase 2 - the experiment continues online

you have the theme
you have the source files
respond
react
create
combine

file-swap with other readers
create hybrids with the artist's works
share inspirations
innovate, experiment

www.friendsofed.com/4x4

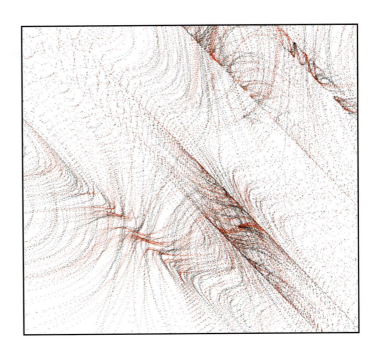

pre-computer:
before i bought my first computer i liked to paint a lot. the most important thing with painting, for me, wasn't working towards an end goal of creating a piece of work which people would want to put on their wall. it was about enjoying the process of experimenting with different colors, materials and techniques. the moment i knew about a certain combination, it became boring and i derived no pleasure from its repetition.

learning:
when i started experimenting with programs on the computer, i soon realized that the opportunities for variation were endless. the moment i became bored with one program, i could switch to another one, and discover what that had to offer. also, with the possibilities that the technology opened up, i could learn a lot in different areas at the same time: about pictures, sound, motion and so on. in the non-digital arena it would have taken me much longer to explore any one of those areas with the same intensity. when i discovered macromedia director, i liked the style of lingo a lot – because of its form. it didn't have too many brackets and points and commas in it. as the non-programmer that i was at the time, that would have immediately scared me away. but it looked to me like some kind of poetry, rather than a programming language.

mathematics:
after i had learned the basics of lingo, i became fascinated by the relationship of pure mathematical formulas, which could be used by lingo, and the visible patterns on the screen that they created.

before that, mathematics seemed to me to be a very dry and useless subject, but i began to change my mind as i discovered more. it can be a way to describe real life (everything which is out there) and also a system of detection to find out more about it.

mathematics can be seen in everything if the mind is focused on it. a tree growing, for instance, can be seen as following a specific pattern, which could also be described in a mathematical way: how big (in meters) can the tree grow (given a range from the minimum to the maximum height)? how many main branches can there be? how many small branches growing out of each big branch? how many leaves or how many blossoms? and so on... in this sense every variable in the growth process can have its own numbers assigned, and is part of a mathematical system. colors and tones represent special frequencies (all of which can be related to each other) and any social aspect can be displayed through numbers as well.

by using a formula to describe a circle, for instance, and making it abstract, you can develop it away from its original purpose. modify the code a little bit here and there, combine different formulas and a new principle can be made visible. perhaps a principle of a certain movement, of attraction or repulsion, or various influences of elements on each other, and so on. this newly developed principle (or the combination of various principles) might already be represented somewhere in nature, but not detected or described by mathematics yet. for me, using mathematics for drawing with lingo is playing around with the visual signals of the code.

nature:
one of the most interesting aspects of using a formula to create something new is that often the result reminds me of something very organic. the symmetry visible in nature is never as exact as it would be if the formula was pursued in pure mathematics. math can come close to nature when you amend the original formula a little bit, or include some random factor.

an example

here is an easy example of a possible evolution from a very strict mathematical grid to a more organic and natural pattern.

100 dots (each consisting of one single black pixel) should be spread across a stage of 100 x 100 pixels:

in picture [01] the distance of the dots from the borders is always 5 pixels and the distance between each point is 10 pixels. the dots are set to very exact positions to form this kind of grid.

in picture [02] the same script is used to set the dots, but the fixed positions of the dots are changed by a random factor: here the dots can either be at the same position as before or at a distance of 1 pixel (horizontally and / or vertically) from their original position. the grid is still easily visible, even though it is already a little distorted.

in picture [03] the maximum possible distance of the dots from their positions in the original grid was set to 4: the basic grid is now not really visible anymore, but it seems as if the dots are still fairly equally spread all over the stage.

in picture [04] the maximum possible distance was set to 15, which makes some dots at the borders disappear from the stage (when the horizontal and vertical values calculated were smaller than 0 or bigger than 100) and mixes the dots up horizontally and vertically: now there is no obvious relation to the original grid at all.

considering the patterns found in plants, the later examples are more easy to find in nature than the first one. the examples [02] – [04] still use the same principle as example [01], but because of the inclusion of the random factor (the "organic factor") the visible results tend to be more realistic in a natural sense. the main principle of spreading the dots equally on the stage (used in all four examples) can also be found in patterns where no grid is visible at first glance (as in example [04]).

numbers, which at first appear to be pure mathematics, can nevertheless be discovered in nature. for instance the numbers of the fibonacci series (where each number is the sum of the previous two: 1 2 3 5 8 13 21 34 55 89 144 233 377 610 987 1597 2584 and so on) can be found in the arrangement of the seeds in a sunflower – though the pattern of a grown sunflower will always look slightly different from a calculation based on the same principle, because it will lack the exactness.

in nature there can be so many different influences on how exactly a plant develops: the seed itself, the ground, the water, the sun, the air, some natural enemies – to name but a few. when modifying the code in a director file, i never know for sure what the result will look like: it is a little bit like planting some mystery seeds and waiting to see what will come out of them. i can influence the results by editing the code – which could be seen as the equivalent of watering the seeds a little bit more or less, or changing some other random factor.

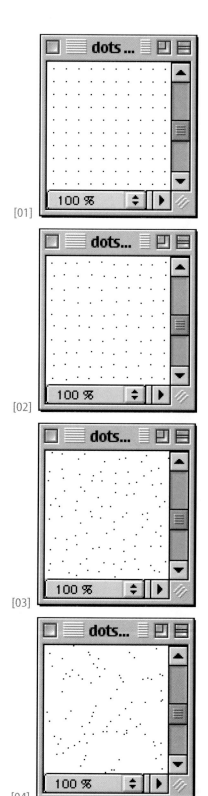

[01]

[02]

[03]

[04]

experiments – applications:

i see my way of working as an experimental process, rather than a set programming method. i never think in advance about each step of the process, because i know that during the work i will come to many points where it will be much more interesting to go in a different direction to the one i had originally planned, or to add something i didn't think about at all in the beginning. of course there has to be a rough idea about what to do in general, but this idea can mainly be seen as the "seed" of the work.

of course it also needs a bit of planning when a work is getting more complex, and the decision has to be taken as to when it should be developed from an experiment to an application. there is also a lot of work to do to make it all functional – which is not so much part of the experimental work, but rather part of the fine-tuning process.

a piece can be self-running, using permanently changing values as the controlling element, or it can be designed to become some kind of drawing tool for other users as well.

if the user is to be able to take an active part in the creation of a picture, then the application needs to enable the user to have an influence in some way. when simply using the mouse-position in relation to the stage dimensions as the only influence, then the connection between the user input of controlling the mouse movement, and the drawn result, is obvious straight away.

of course the application can also contain much more complexity – with various possibilities for the user to influence the drawing process. these additional possibilities could for instance include:

• checking for rollovers

• checking the mouse-position in relation to the moving elements themselves – which can determine a wide range of definitions (like the size, the color, the blend, the shape of those elements and so on).

• offering buttons to click, which can directly change small parts of the code used.

the more complex the method, the more difficult it becomes for users to discover how to exert control over what comes out at the end. in this sense i see such a ready-made application as a sort of game, where the "rules" are only detected step by step (like going to another level of experience). as more rules are recognized by the user, more creative possibilities become apparent.

as i like users to have a similar experience of detecting functionality when playing around with the application as i do when programming it, i avoid defining how the pieces themselves should be used. i think that this can make discovering them a more playful experience: instead of having a fixed manual and just trying to achieve the same results as someone else did before, there should be an absolute freedom for research. for me it is important that some time is spent exploring the pieces: the user should be able to create their own method of using the application, to create an independent result. sometimes, after having played around extensively with an application myself during its development, i have been genuinely astonished by how different the results can be when someone else uses it!

i see early pieces i did on turux (http://www.turux.org) more as experiments than as finished applications:

in the following piece for instance (number 09 in block 01 in the current menu of turux) no interactivity was programmed at all – the user can only watch as the piece develops a picture during runtime.

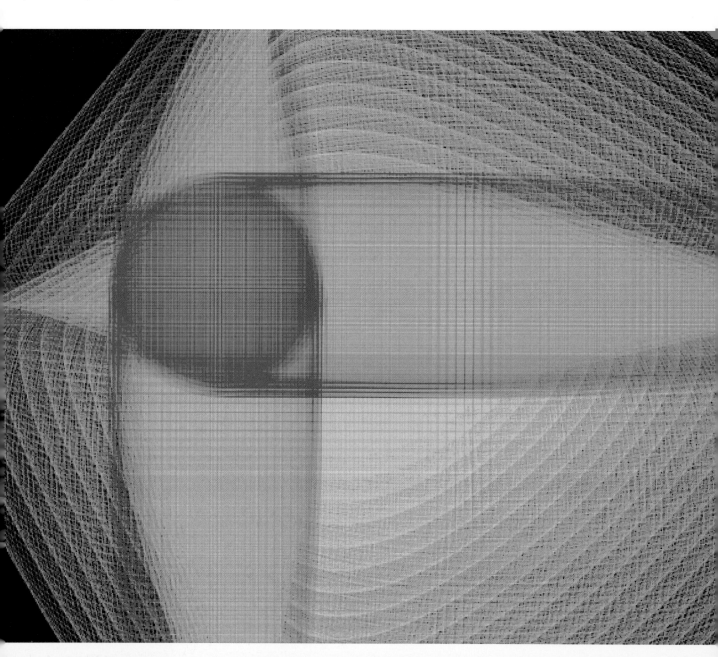

i see the works i put on re-move (http://www.re-move.org) more as applications, because they contain more complexity, and interactivity is possible. there are lots of different buttons to be explored, which allow the user much more control over the creation of a picture:

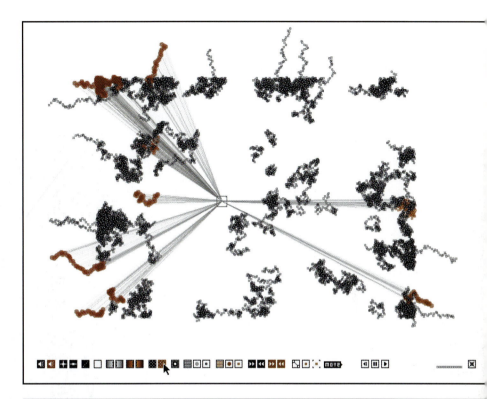

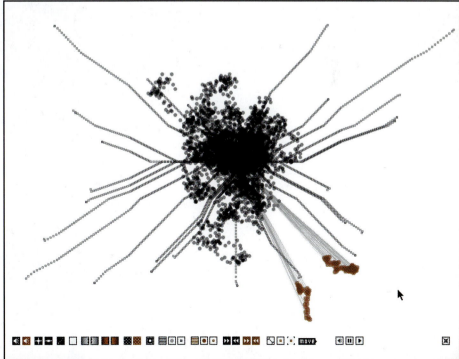

inspiration:

inspiration can be very hard to pin down. as mathematics can be seen behind so many things, the sources which give the main inspiration for a piece can be varied. "real" things like the growing pattern of a plant, for instance, or a photo of a physical experiment, or more "abstract" things like different emotions, dreams, or observations of social principles. sometimes i only get the full idea of a principle after i have been trying to translate it into lingo and have succeeded in making it visible for myself. before that the ideas can be too vague to be made definite. keeping ideas open often allows more complex structures to evolve out of the process.

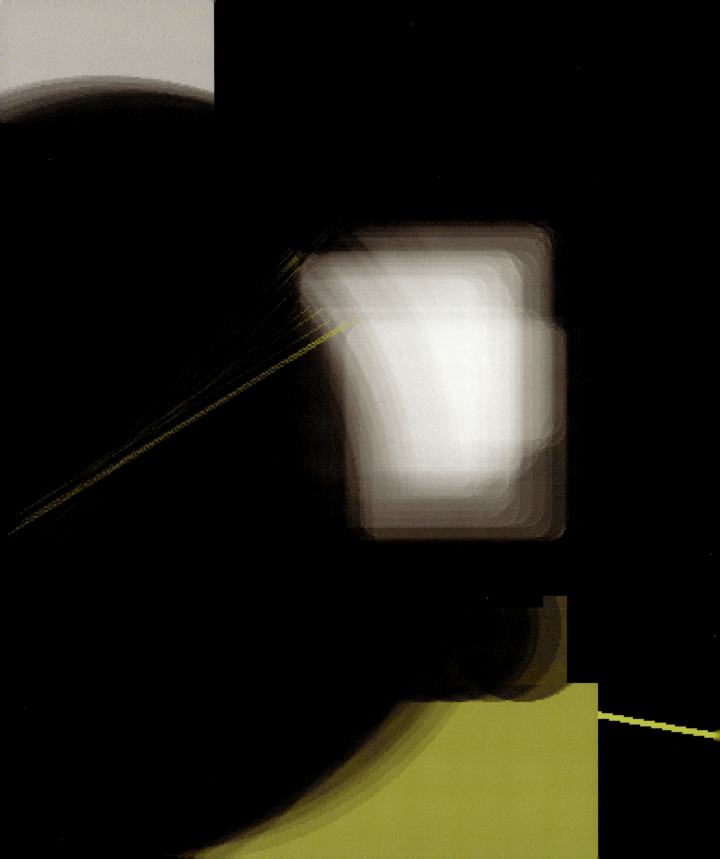

influences / collaborations:

since i started working with computers, in vienna, i have met several people who work in similar fields. because working processes in different areas (like music, video, graphic design, architecture, programming and so on) are increasingly merging together through the use of computers, most of these people are busy with more than one discipline.

it is almost impossible to say one influence was more important than another, because i think that people are constantly influencing each other – it is like having a never ending dialogue. also, whether the information you receive will become an important influence or not depends on it being the right time for you. also the influence which the people in vienna had on me was not only through their works, but also through meeting them in person.

here i just want to list a selection of web-pages which show some of the work of those people and groups (in the approximate order i got to know them / their work):

http://www.dextro.org (dextro)

http://www.werke-dd.co.at (richard miklos)

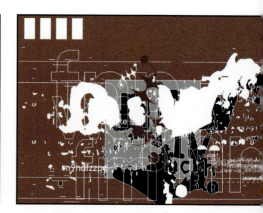

http://www.farmersmanual.co.at

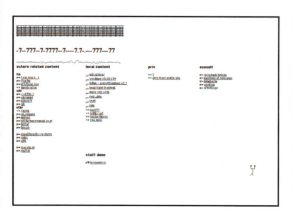

http://0zombie.test.at (ost)

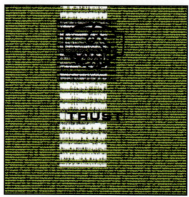

http://trust.at (glow)

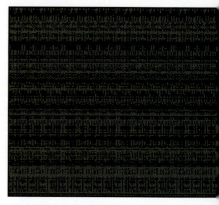

http://pure.test.at (pure)

http://snudd.sil.at (stephan possert)

http://datadouche.web.fm (hiaz)

http://www.frank.at (tina frank)

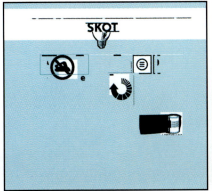

http://www.skot.at

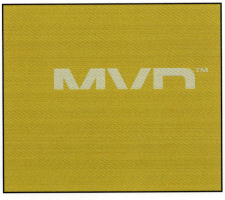

http://www.mvd.org

http://www.fals.ch

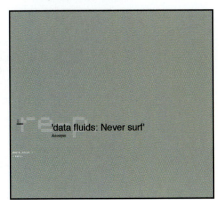

http://www.re-p.at
http://www.vidok.org

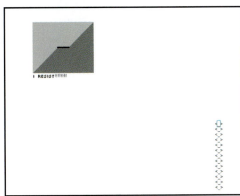

http://www.notdef.org (maia)

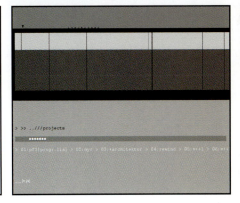

http://www.n-ja.org (n:ja)

i have collaborated with some of these people during the past few years, some others have just influenced my own work through their style of working.

in the beginning, i learned a lot from dextro – mainly the basic usage of the computer and about an alternative way that computer-graphics could look.

in 1997 we started the web-project www.turux.org, which is a collection of experiments in the director shockwave format.

one of the works i like the most there is the one (number 0404 in the menu) which was created for the fourth issue of the japanese series *gasbook*:

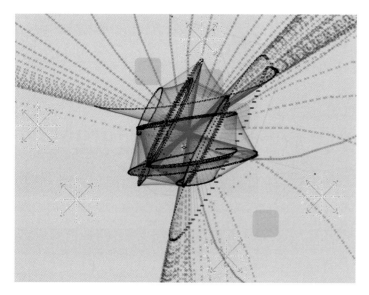 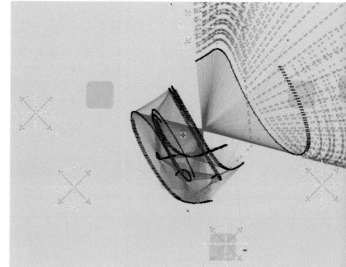

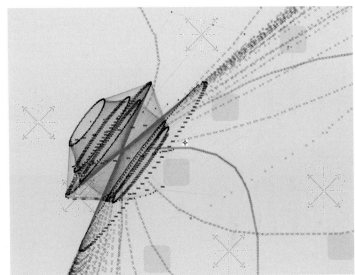

another project on turux contains pieces which were created for an installation in the klangturm st.pölten near vienna (in block number 03 in the menu). a 3d-script (written by che tamahori: http://www.sfx.co.nz/tamahori/thought/shock_3d_howto.html) was used to create objects which could be used to control different sounds, which were connected to the endpoints (corners) of those objects. at the installation there were two connected computers running with these applications so that two people could mix their sounds together at the same time.

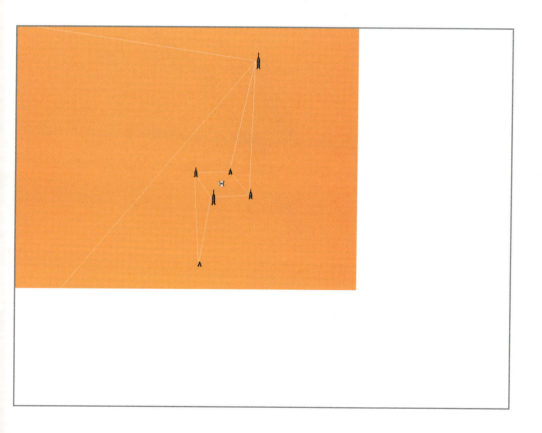

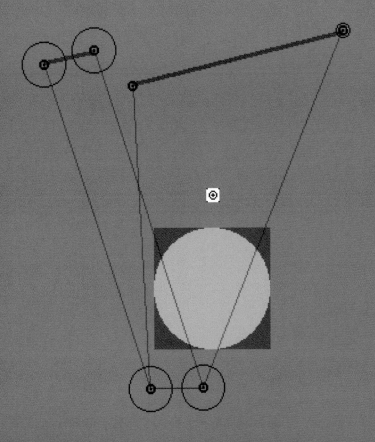

another project was with maia (www.re-p.at, www.nietdelli.org) and nija (www.ii-ja.org).

it was for an exhibition in brazil which was called www.mycity.com.br and which showed pieces from 46 different countries.

the brief was to create a piece which would represent the city you were living in. In this work every one of us did everything: creating pictures, programming, sounds and so on. the viennese map gets enlarged in a small rectangle to the side of it. whenever a white dot is discovered with the "magnifying lens" something is displayed on the right side which we thought fitted that specific area/place of the city.

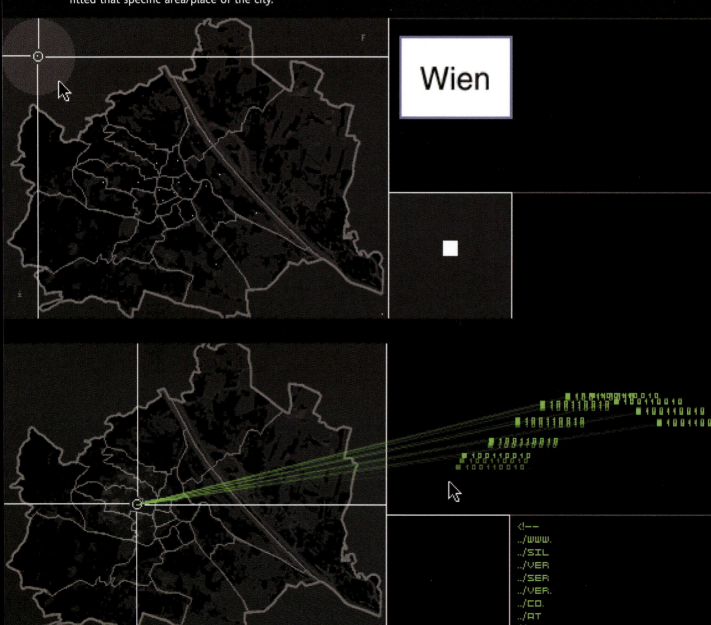

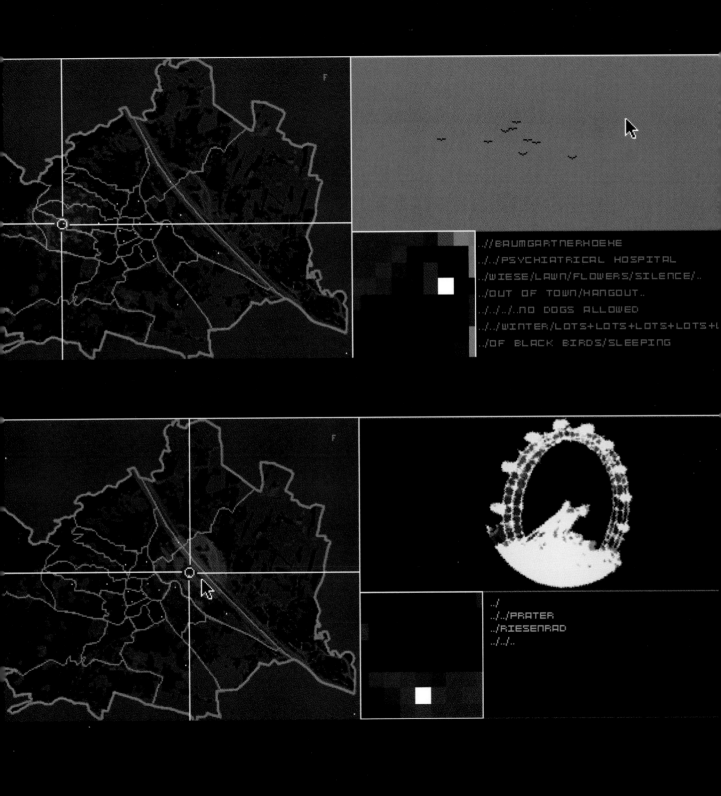

..//BAUMGARTNERHOEHE
../../PSYCHIATRICAL HOSPITAL
../WIESE/LAWN/FLOWERS/SILENCE/..
./OUT OF TOWN/HANGOUT..
../../../..NO DOGS ALLOWED
../../WINTER/LOTS+LOTS+LOTS+LOTS+L
./OF BLACK BIRDS/SLEEPING

../
../../PRATER
../RIESENRAD
../../.

notes 01 was another collaboration between norbert pfaffenpichler and me. it was done for the online-project called v++ (http://www.thing.at/v++/notes.html).

the initial idea came from norbert and he also provided me with most of the pictures. my part was officially "programming the whole thing" but i see programming also as a very creative process. it is only after some ideas have been translated to the programming language and have become visible, that the dead ends become clear and new ideas and new directions can be developed.

collaborations with people living in vienna are not just restricted to internet projects, i also did some real-time visuals to the live music produced by pure (http://pure.test.at) at a project called *live_forms* in front of the museumsquartier in vienna (june 2001). the fun of doing live visuals is that i never know in advance what exactly will come out of it. the necessary materials can be prepared before, but later on this material can be used in many different ways. pictures of that event can be seen at http://www.lanolin.at.

at the moment i'm working very closely with revdesign (http://www.revdesign.pt) located in portugal:

REV DESIGN LDA   NEW//

++351 223.714.254
++FAX 223.714.255
WWW.REVDESIGN.PT
DESIGN@REVDESIGN.PT

CARVALHAIS@REVDESIGN.PT
SALAZAR@REVDESIGN.PT

2001 381
2001 @EXD2001
2001 FB56

TRY//

> WWW.ANANANA.PT
> WWW.CHEYENNE-PT.COM
> WWW.CURTASMETRAGENS.PT
  .../AGENCIA
  .../FESTIVAL
  .../GERAÇÃO CURTAS
> WWW.DE-GAME.ORG
> WWW.EXPERIMENTADESIGN.PT
> WWW.FORCE-INC.NET
> WWW.FORCE-TRACKS.NET
> WWW.MAJORELECTRICO.NET
> WWW.MILLE-PLATEAUX.NET
> WWW.POSITION-CHROME.NET
> WWW.RITORNELL.NET
> WWW.WHO.PT
> ZZZZZZZZZZZZZZZZZP.ORG

ARCHIVE//

2001 AJANELA.COM
2000 LUXFRAGIL.COM
2000 WWR3Y
2000 SISTER SPACES (SAN FRANCISCO)
  ——— REV + MAJOR ELÉCTRICO
  ——— MAJOR ELÉCTRICO + REV
1999 EXPERIMENTADESIGN99
1999 HOUSEWARE EXPERIENCE
1998 REVVOLVER
1995 UP-ARTE

OFF//

2001 CURTAS 9 VILA [
2001 MEIA CAVE 16Y
2001 SHORTS GENERA
2001 CLICKS & CUTS 2
2001 CHEYENNE S/S 2
2001 RANDOM_INC : JE
2001 BLAAST
2001 GOODBYE MEIA (
2000 XMASMSG
2000 CHEYENNE A/W (
1999 IN THE FUTURE E
1999 INSTANTES
1999 PRIDE
1998 ONDAS MARTEN
1998 1Y
1996 [UP]ARTE 2

20011009

with revdesign, i was asked to do a redesign for a german music label (www.force-inc.net, www.force-tracks.net, www.mille-plateaux.net, www.position-chrome.net, www.ritornell.net). for me it was actually the first time that i did "real" graphic design for a client. we were very lucky in this case, because on the one hand the client just allowed us almost everything we wanted to do, and on the other hand they provided us with "real" content (not like many other companies which just want to have a "good looking" webpage without any content). many of the background-pictures used for this website were generated using macromedia director.

director was also used for the production of the main material for the revdesign cover of *clicks & cuts 2* (released on mille-plateaux). in this case i'm rather proud that i solved the problem with the low resolution of screen-design (72 dpi): the director application i did for that had 7680 x 4096 pixel (more were not possible due to a lack of memory) and numbers from 1 to 24 were set on the 24 sections of this screen (to keep the overview). with the arrow keys i could move the big application around on the screen, making another section visible and good for a screenshot. after taking 24 different screenshots i reassembled them to make one single big picture, which could then be used for print at a higher resolution.

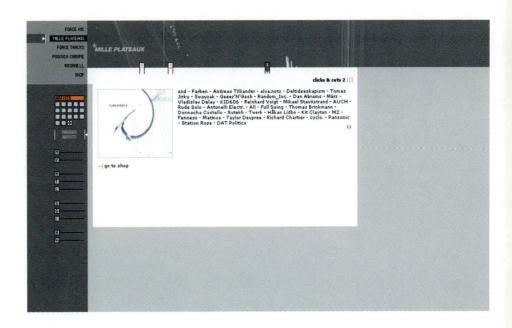

as for the work for the tutorial in this book, a spirograph drawing machine – found at a flea market – was my main source of inspiration. i basically wanted to show the steps of a possible working process:

• getting a rough idea about which principle should become visible

• starting with the translation of this principle into lingo

• experimenting with the code

of course in this case i tried to keep things as simple as possible, so that the sense of the development process could be clear.

this piece should basically work as an example of how mathematics can be used within director using lingo to make some principles visible – and it is not really finished yet, in the sense of being a ready-made application. the code in this case could still grow in many different directions. for instance in the beginning i thought about creating the possibility (in the script called circ2) of allowing the dots to move in an elliptical path as well as a circular one. later on i decided that i wouldn't like to include this feature in this piece yet, but i left the code in there for eventual further use. also the use of the single-pixel cast member was intended to show the exact movements that the code is prescribing: for the development of a more aesthetically pleasing drawing i would continue to try out different elements to make up the final drawing – by either adding pixels to "dot" or by using some vector shapes or shapes from the tool palette (rectangle, round rectangle, ellipse). it could also be interesting to extend the application further than merely a visual level by including some sound – which could give more feedback on how the code is working, and in this way help the user to understand it better and to develop it in another direction. in this way the application could also be functional as some kind of instrument, rather than just as a drawing tool.

the piece discussed in the book is intended as an inspirational source for the thoughts and experiments of the reader: it should be clear that there are no fixed rules at all. how different formulas should be used or abused, or which principle (detected or created) is worth being taken further, is completely up to the user. also the final choice of components used (the colors, the shapes and so forth) will always be dependent on an individual's sense of aesthetics.

what i hope to achieve with my work, in general, is to show how beautiful mathematics can be when depicted. maybe it's only a matter of being patient enough to experiment until the right numbers can be found in the code (by trial and error) which then make the natural aesthetics of formulas apparent. programming sometimes means to me bringing to life my own "creatures" (with some added behaviors) and then watching how they act on the screen until they fall back into oblivion. i see programming as a continuous process, where only parts of the code will "survive" when being reused by another piece of work.

i think that the process of my work is not so much about using an existing knowledge of mathematics, but more about acquiring knowledge of it through experimentation.

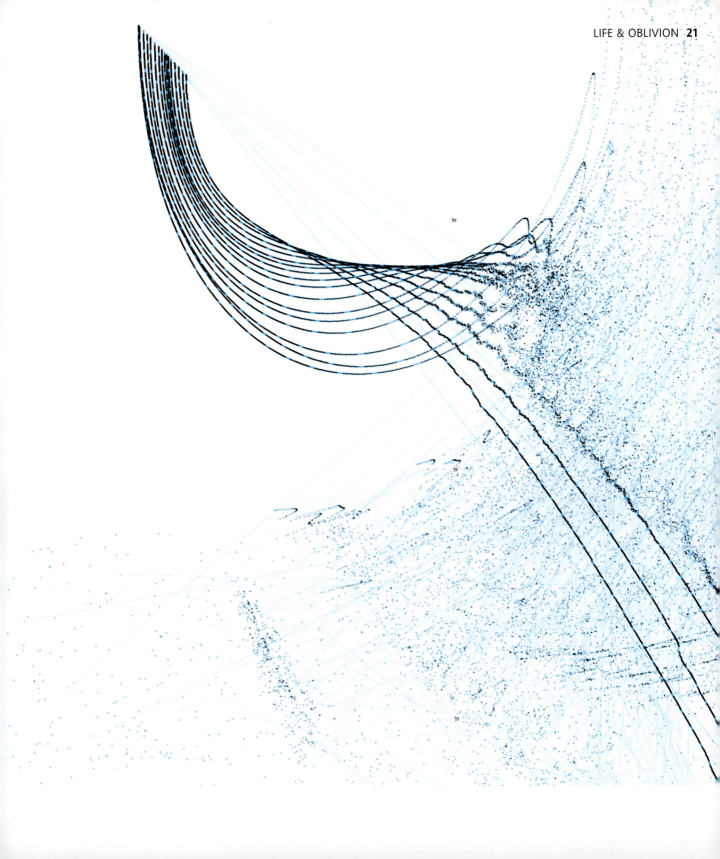

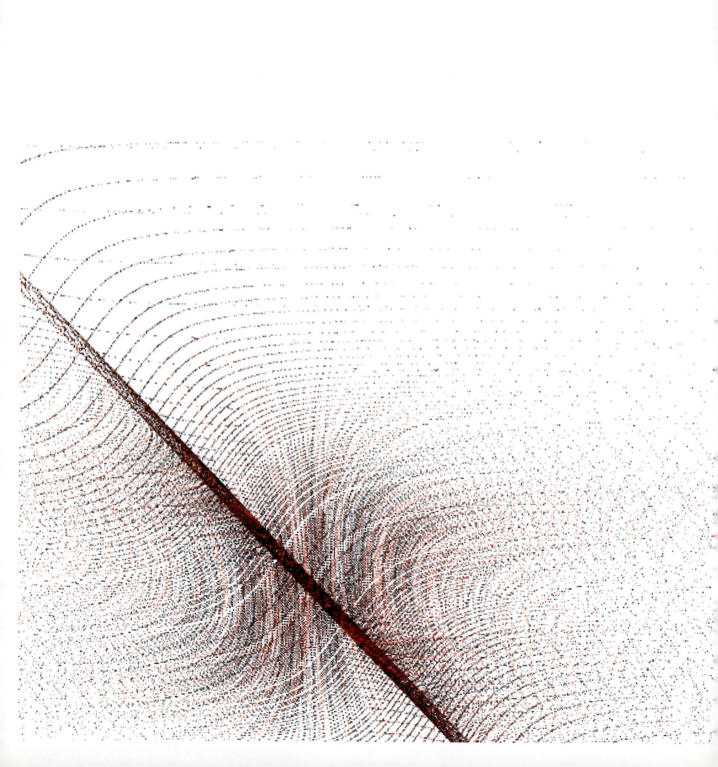

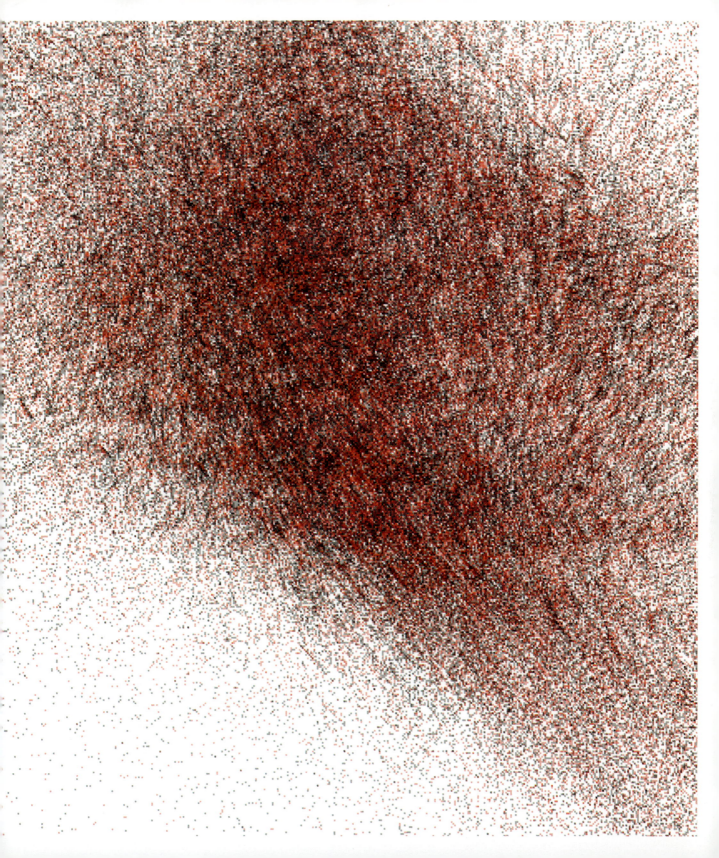

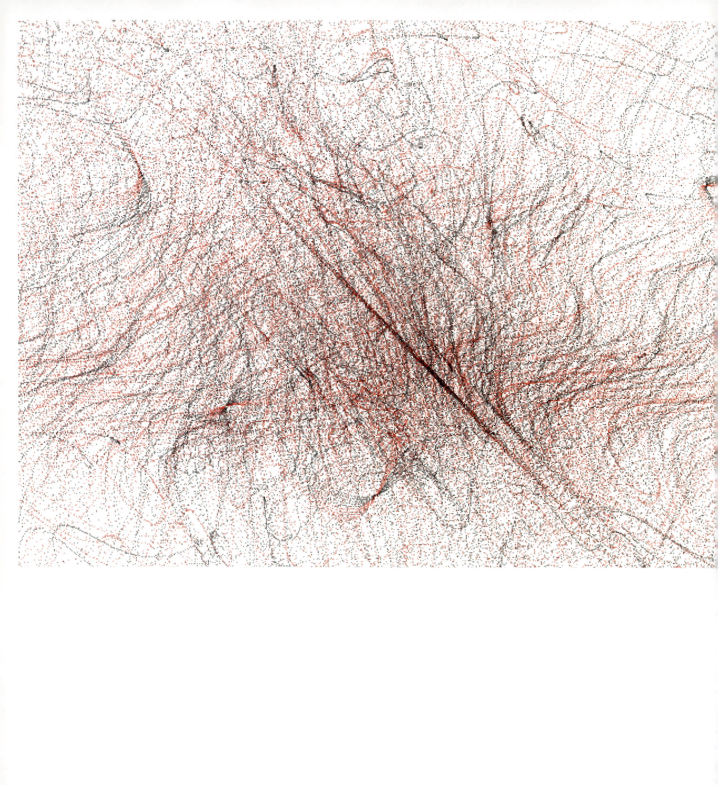

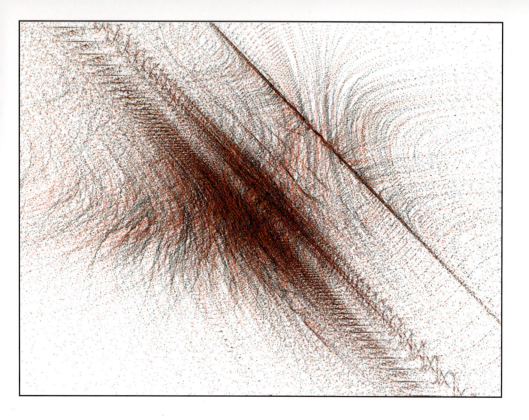

The following piece will be created in Macromedia Director 8.5 – using its programming language, Lingo.

When I started learning Director, it was mainly used for creating interactive, easy to navigate showcases. But I soon realized I was much more interested in creating something using and displaying mathematical functions, rather than simply creating some highlighted buttons or moving pictures. At high school I wasn't very good at mathematics, but through learning Lingo I discovered a new fascination for all those rules and formulas, and the unexpected results that can be created with them.

My work process can be reduced to a few steps:

Discovering a principle which I think could be interesting to play around with in a mathematical way.

Putting together the main necessary scripts in Lingo.

Tweaking these scripts by changing or adding small parts of code (like a plus or a minus sign for instance) and reacting to the results.

Inspiration – the mathematical principle

Searching for some ideas for this project, I found inspiration at a flea market near Vienna.

Besides various pens and several sheets of paper, this box also contained a drawing machine with three drawing wheels.

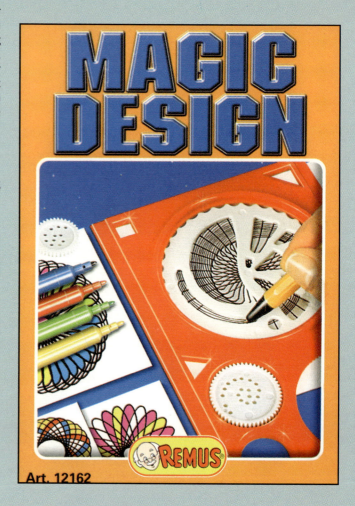

Art. 12162

The main principle of using this tool to create Magic Design is rotation:

As you can see from the shots of the packaging, the big white gear wheel has various openings in it, of different shapes and sizes, whereas the two smaller wheels have a series of small round holes. The user puts one of the pens into one of these holes, and applies pressure to rotate the drawing wheel around the inner edge of an opening in the red plastic base shape.

As the white wheel is being thrust around within the red base, a number of different movements occur simultaneously to generate the distinctive pattern.

The center of the white wheel is describing a circle – the center of this circle is at the same point as the center of the hole in the base. Obviously, as the white wheel is rotating, any point on it is also describing a perfect circle. However, these circles do not relate to the center hole in the red plastic base.

For its part, the big wheel has various shaped openings, which cause a repeated pattern of this shape to be drawn as the wheel rotates. To get an idea of what kind of drawings can be created using these wheels, some "machine-drawn" pictures are shown, right.

The first two were created using the medium sized wheel. I used a different hole for each drawing, one nearer the center and one closer to the edge. The third was created with the biggest wheel, using the largest shaped hole.

After having considered the different kinds of movement that come into play as these geometrical patterns are produced, it's time to start thinking about translating it to Lingo. Thinking about translating the main principle into Lingo is not so much about trying to create exactly the same results you get with the drawing machine, but more about discovering what else might be done with the underlying idea. Let's begin by firing up Macromedia Director 8.5.

The first thing to do is to change the preferences. This is not mandatory but it might be helpful to synchronize watches, so to speak. It will make it easier to compare the screenshots, and will hopefully avoid any erratic Director-type behavior.

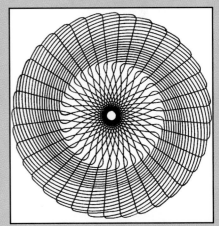

File > Preferences > Score

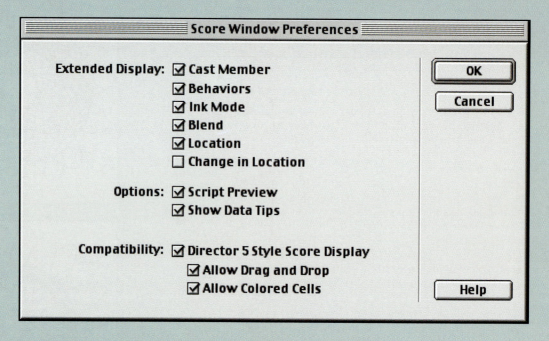

Checking Script Preview extends the score and a field appears above the channels. This is useful in two ways. It displays a preview of the assigned scripts when you click on the sprites in the channels. It can also be used to access the scripts to make direct changes to them.

Checking Director 5 Style Score Display shows the cast member numbers of the sprites in the score, instead of bars (provided all preferences are set as detailed opposite). This setting is also available if you ctrl-click / right-click in the frame bar of the score window.

instead of

File > Preferences > Sprite

If the Span Duration is set to 1 then every time a cast member is dragged onto the stage or into the score, the sprite does not extend over more than one frame.

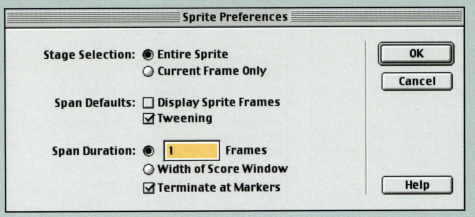

File > Preferences > Cast

Thumbnail Size set to Small allows you to have more cast members visible in the Cast Window at the same time.

Label set to Number:Name shows the cast member number and name below each cast member in the Cast Window, and it shows the cast member numbers in the score.

File > Preferences > Editors

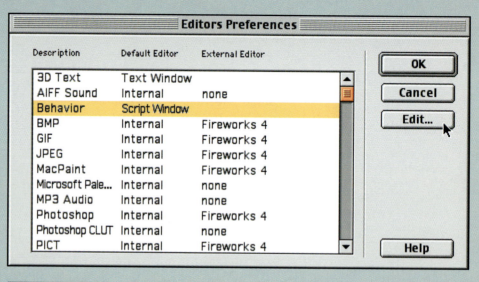

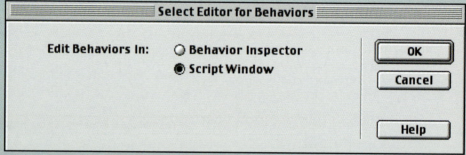

When Edit Behaviors In is set to Script Window then every time you double-click on a script cast member the editable script itself is immediately opened, rather than the Behavior Inspector.

View > Sprite Toolbar

This extends the score, showing the same information as the Sprite Property Inspector. A small preview picture and script is visible in the score window, along with several fields and buttons to use when changing attributes of the sprite.

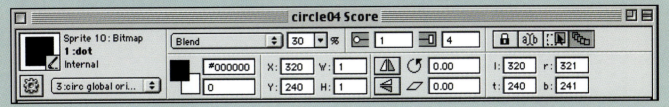

View > Sprite Overlay > Show Info – uncheck !!!

Having the Show Info preference enabled, Director would draw a rectangle below each selected sprite containing some information about that sprite.

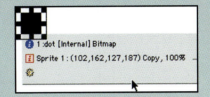

View > Sprite Overlay > Show Paths – uncheck !!!

With Show Paths checked, Director would draw a line where a sprite moves over several frames in the score.

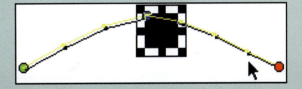

The various windows in Director can be made visible or invisible by clicking them in Window >, or by pressing the key combination written there.

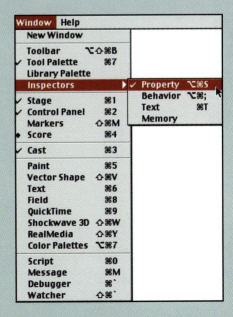

With the items above checked, the following windows
should be visible on the screen:

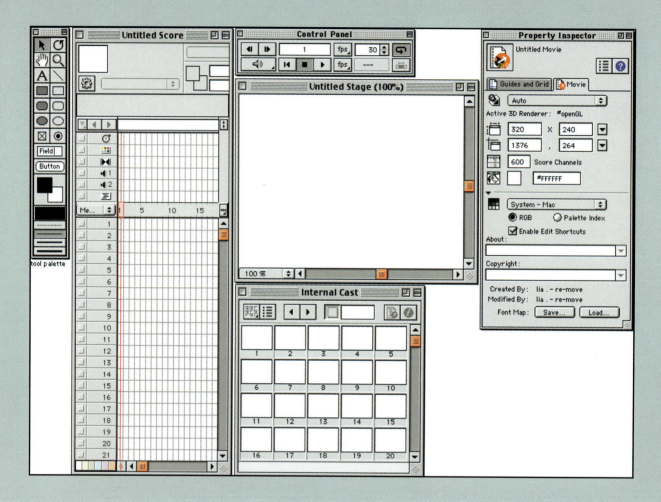

Note that the content of the Property Inspector changes,
depending on which is active. (Click on a window to make
it active.)

Setting up the movie

Create a new movie, and save it as circles01.

To define the size and color of the stage, you should click on the stage window. It will become active and that ensure the Property Inspector is displaying the correct screen.

So, select Windows > Inspectors > Property. Click on the Movie Properties tab in the Property Inspector. I chose 640 x 480 pixels for this piece. This is a standard size in Director and as such it can be chosen from the popup menu beside the two fields for the stage size. The stage color can be set to white by holding down the mouse on the rectangle beside the Stage Fill Color icon.

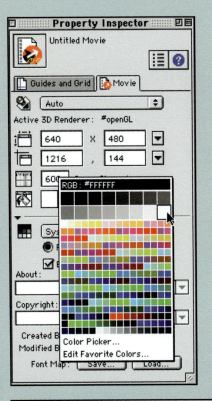

Designing a character

Now we've got the preferences sorted, we'll begin creating a character. This will be something visible on stage which can be used to track the programmed movements. It is good to start with a very small drawing in the Paint Window, which can be accessed via Window > Paint. Create a very small square, like I have in the screenshot. Mine is a small black square, 3x3 pixels, drawn with the pencil, and it is named dot. This name can be typed into the Cast Member Name field at the top of the Paint Window.

To get an enlarged view select the Magnifying Glass in the toolbar of the Paint Window, and click in the window several times. You can zoom out by holding down the shift button and clicking. To return to normal view click once on the rectangle containing the 100% view of the image in the Paint area. Alternatively you can use the shortcut keys whilst using the drawing tools, ctrl + / ctrl –, to zoom in and out.

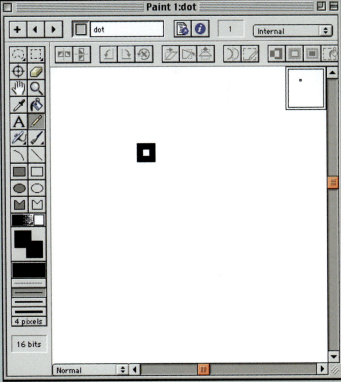

Now you can close the Paint Window, and open the cast window (Window > Cast). You can now make the new cast member visible on the stage by dragging it from the cast window into the 10th channel of the score. Any other channel could be chosen for this, but sometimes it's a good idea to keep the first few channels free, just in case you need to add some more sprites later on, which need to appear behind the first one. (Note that, unless you employ a bit of Lingo trickery, the topmost sprite on the stage is the one with the highest channel number).

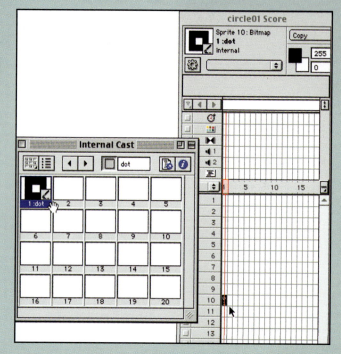

To make the sprite containing dot also available in the next two frames, the first three frames in channel 10 should be selected. (Hold down Shift to select more than one frame by clicking).

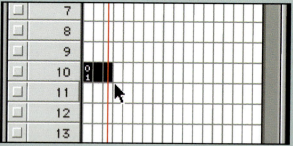

Then, select Modify > Extend Sprite.

This extension of the sprite will enable us to loop the movie in frame 3 in a moment. Frame 3 is selected here for a similar reason as channel 10 was selected before: to keep free space for the possibility of other scripts being executed before the loop in frame 3 starts.

Okay, let's look at looping the movie.

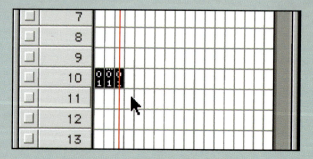

We will write a framescript in frame 3 which will cause the header to loop in frame 3. This will make Lingo – written in an `on exitFrame` handler – continue permanently as long as the movie is running. This is needed to make some calculations for movements later on.

First off we need to add a frame script in frame 3. Above the gray numbered timeline you should see a series of rows with icons (if you can't, try pressing the Hide/Show Effects Channels button on the right of the timeline). On the Script Channel, go to frame 3 and double-click.

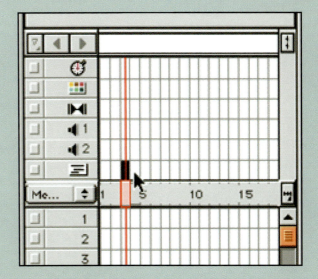

This will bring up the Script Window. The Behavior Script should be named `looper`, in the Cast Member Name box at the top of the window.

Type `go the frame` and delete the word `me` from the pre-written code, so the Behavior Script window looks like this:

Now, when you run the movie for the first time, using the controls in the control panel, the header will loop in frame 3.

This is not a very visible loop in the sense of being able to see the header moving around, but the header is permanently exiting frame 3 and – because of the line `go the frame` inside the `on exitFrame` handler – it is immediately re-entering frame 3. The time used for one loop depends on the Frames Per Second settings for the movie, which at default is 30 fps.

Movement 1

Now we must turn our attention to getting some movement in a circle. To make our little dot move on the stage, we need to assign a Behavior Script to the sprite in channel 10 (containing the dot cast member).

Select the entire sprite over all three frames. After clicking into the Script Preview area of the score, a new script window will be opened. Note – if you do not see the Script Preview area, try ctrl-click or right-click. This should solve any problems!

Call the Behavior Script circ. We are going to type the following Lingo into this script window:

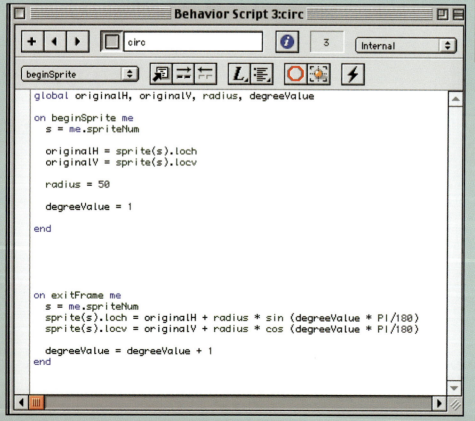

```
global originalH, originalV, radius, degreeValue

on beginSprite me
  s = me.spriteNum

  originalH = sprite(s).loch
  originalV = sprite(s).locv

  radius = 50

  degreeValue = 1

end




on exitFrame me
  s = me.spriteNum
  sprite(s).loch = originalH + radius * sin (degreeValue * PI/180)
  sprite(s).locv = originalV + radius * cos (degreeValue * PI/180)

  degreeValue = degreeValue + 1
end
```

The first line sets to `global` the variables `originalH, originalV, radius` and `degreeValue`. If a variable is set to `global` at the top of a script window, then the values assigned to this variable can be accessed in every handler in this script, simply by using its name. So far there are two handlers, `on beginSprite` and `on exitFrame`. The variables with their assigned values can also be used in a different script (written in a different script window) if they are also set to `global` at the top of this new script.

In the `on beginSprite` handler all the initial values are defined. The line `s = me.spriteNum` gives the variable named `s` the value of the number of the sprite to which this script is assigned, in this case the value 10, because it is on the tenth channel.

The first time the header in the score enters any frame containing the sprite (with this script assigned to it) all Lingo in this `on beginSprite` handler is executed once.

Here the current position of sprite 10 (in this case the center of the stage, because it was dragged into the score, and director automatically centers it on the stage when doing so) is recorded and assigned to the two variables, `originalH`, which is equal to the horizontal location, 320 pixels, and `originalV` which is equal to the vertical location, 240 pixels.

The variable called `radius` is given the value 50. The bigger this value, the bigger the radius of the circle described by sprite 10 will be.

The `degreeValue` here is set to 1, to start the movement at 1 degree. One full rotation of sprite 10 in a circle would go from 1 to 360 degrees.

In the `on exitFrame` handler the movement of sprite 10 in a circle is defined.

```
s = me.spriteNum
```

Here the variable `s` again has the sprite number assigned to it, 10.

```
sprite(s).loch = originalH + radius * sin (degreeValue * PI/180)
sprite(s).locv = originalV + radius * cos (degreeValue * PI/180)
```

Each time the header exits (loops in) frame 3, `sprite(s).loch` is the new horizontal location of sprite 10, and `sprite(s).locv` is the new vertical location.

These two lines of code are using the original centerpoint of sprite 10 (`originalH, originalV`) as the centerpoint of the circle that sprite 10 will describe. The variables `originalH` and `originalV` were already assigned values in the `on beginSprite` handler, 320 and 240, and because they were set to be `global` variables at the top of the script, they can be reused here.

```
radius * sin (degreeValue * PI/180)
radius * cos (degreeValue * PI/180)
```

These parts of the code are calculating the values for setting the new position of sprite 10 to a point on the circumference of a circle with a radius of 50 and with the centerpoint using the values of `originalH` and `originalV`. The location on this circumference depends on the value assigned to the variable `degreeValue`.

```
degreeValue = degreeValue + 1
```

This value is permanently increasing by 1 each time the header exits the frame. Where the variable `degreeValue` is set from 1 to 360, one full rotation is described, then from 361 to 720 the next revolution is completed, and so on.

Press play here on the controller to see what we have created so far.

Using this formula, sprite moves 10 circles counter-clockwise around its original position, 50 pixels out, and using 360 steps to describe a full circle.

To see what's happening on the stage more clearly, you can give the moving sprite Trails. To do so, select the sprite in all frames, and then check the Trails button in the Property Inspector.

On the stage, this shows the sprite at all the positions it has moved through. Now, if you play the movie again, the trails of sprite 10 will draw a simple circle on the stage.

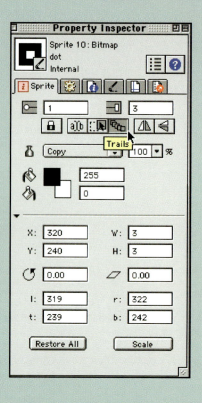

Movement 2

Okay, let's get to creating a more general behavior. Up until now, the movement created with sprite 10 describes the same movement as the center of the white wheel on our drawing machine did, when it was dragged around in the red base shape.

For the approximation of the second movement – the rotation of the white shape around its own cycling center – our code needs an additional behavior, using the first rotating sprite as its centerpoint.

To save time and scripting, we can create a more general behavior, which can be reused for any sprite. This behavior gives the possibility of changing the different initial values immediately when assigning the script to the sprite – for instance choosing which sprite's location should be used as a center point, the value of the radius or the speed of movement. First duplicate the cast member circ. To do this, select the cast member in the cast window by clicking on it, copy it, select an empty cast member by clicking at the bottom of the list in the Internal Cast window, and paste.

Rename the duplicate circ2 and modify the code as follows. (Note – make sure it's circ2 you're modifying, as mistakes are easy to make and hard to rectify!)

```
╔═══════════════════════════ Behavior Script 4:circ2 ═══════════════════════╗
║ □                                                                  ▣ ▤ ║
║ ┌─┬─┬─┐  ┌──┐ ┌──────────────────────────────────┐  ┌─┐  ┌─┐ ┌──────────┬─┐ ║
║ │+│◄│►│  │□ │ │ circ2                            │  │ⓘ│  │4│ │ Internal │▼│ ║
║ └─┴─┴─┘  └──┘ └──────────────────────────────────┘  └─┘  └─┘ └──────────┴─┘ ║
║ ┌──────────┬─┐                                                               ║
║ │ [global] │▼│  [icons]                                                      ║
║ └──────────┴─┘                                                               ║
║ ┌─────────────────────────────────────────────────────────────────────┐▲    ║
║ │ global degreeVal                                                     │     ║
║ │ property centerPointSprite, centerH, centerV, radiusH, radiusV, speed│     ║
║ │                                                                      │     ║
║ │ on beginSprite me                                                    │     ║
║ │   centerH = sprite(centerPointSprite).loch                           │     ║
║ │   centerV = sprite(centerPointSprite).locv                           │     ║
║ │   degreeVal = 1                                                       │     ║
║ │ end                                                                  │     ║
║ │                                                                      │     ║
║ │ on exitFrame me                                                      │     ║
║ │   s = me.spriteNum                                                   │     ║
║ │                                                                      │     ║
║ │   centerH = sprite(centerPointSprite).loch                           │     ║
║ │   centerV = sprite(centerPointSprite).locv                           │     ║
║ │                                                                      │     ║
║ │   sprite(s).loch = centerH + radiusH * sin (degreeVal * speed * PI/180)│    ║
║ │   sprite(s).locv = centerV + radiusV * cos (degreeVal * speed * PI/180)│    ║
║ │                                                                      │     ║
║ │   degreeVal = degreeVal + 1                                          │     ║
║ │ end                                                                  │     ║
║ │                                                                      │     ║
║ │ on getPropertyDescriptionList me                                     │     ║
║ │   pList = [:]                                                        │     ║
║ │   pList.addProp(#centerPointSprite, [#default: 10, #format: #integer, #comment: "center_sprite ?"])│
║ │   pList.addProp(#radiusH, [#default: 50, #format: #integer, #comment: "radius_h ?"])│
║ │   pList.addProp(#radiusV, [#default: 50, #format: #integer, #comment: "radius_v ?"])│
║ │   pList.addProp(#speed, [#default: 1.00, #format: #float, #comment: "speed ?"])│
║ │   return pList                                                       │     ║
║ │ end                                                                  │▼    ║
║ └─────────────────────────────────────────────────────────────────────┘     ║
╚═══════════════════════════════════════════════════════════════════════════╝
```

At the beginning of the script various properties are defined:

```
global degreeVal
property centerPointSprite, centerH, centerV, radiusH, radiusV, speed
```

In the on beginSprite handler the variable degreeVal is assigned a value. It is used here in the same way as the variable called degreeValue in the previous script circ: it is permanently increasing and also causing the actual movement on the circumference.

Two other variables are defined in the on beginSprite handler:

```
centerH = sprite(centerPointSprite).loch
centerV = sprite(centerPointSprite).locv
```

Here the horizontal and vertical positions of the center sprite are assigned to the variables centerH and centerV.
In the on exitFrame handler these two variables get new (different) values, every time the header exits and re-enters the frame.

These two variables are used again in the next two lines as giving the values for the centerpoint of the rotation:

```
sprite(s).loch = centerH + radiusH * sin (degreeVal * speed * PI/180)
sprite(s).locv = centerV + radiusV * cos (degreeVal * speed * PI/180)
```

These two lines basically work like the similar lines in the circ script: they move the sprite (with this script attached) on a circular path. The difference here is, each time this script is assigned to a sprite, the values of the properties `centerPointSprite, radiusH, radiusV, speed` can be different for each sprite (depending on which values are typed into the fields of the popup window, as explained below.)

The property `speed` is used to speed up or slow down the movement as it is used for multiplying the value of the variable `degreeVal` in the formula.

In the `on getPropertyDescriptionList` handler a property list is created, named `pList`. Several properties are defined there and added to this list:

    #centerPointSprite, #radiusH, #radiusV, #speed

This handler causes a popup window to be opened every time the script `circ2` is attached to a sprite and allows you to assign different values to these properties (which can be different for each sprite)

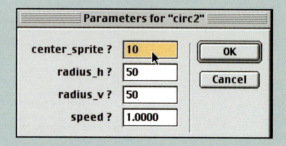

So let's get to creating that second movement on screen.

To create a second dot circling around the first one, select the `dot` cast member and drag it into channel 11, then extend it as before, so that it is extended over the first 3 frames. The ready written behavior `circ2` can now be assigned to sprite 11, either by dragging cast member 4, which contains the script `circ2`, over sprite 11 or by preselecting sprite 11 in the Score and choosing the script out of the Behaviors context menu in the sprite toolbar in the Score window.

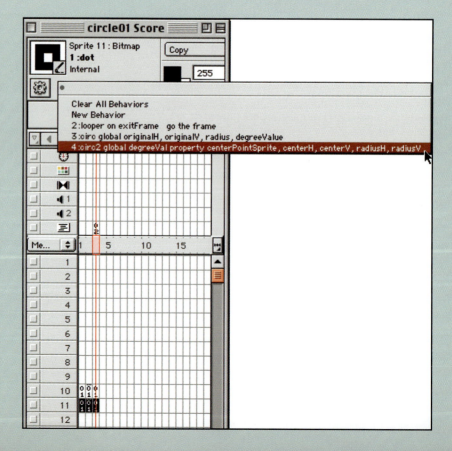

In the popup window, which appears when you attach this Behavior, you can now select different values for the properties of sprite 11. For the time being, we will mainly use the default values.

```
center_sprite ? 10
radius_h ? 50
radius_v ? 50
speed ? 1.00
```

In this case sprite 10 is selected, by typing in the number 10, to be the center of the circle which sprite 11 should describe. The horizontal radius remains at 50, as does the vertical radius – if both values are the same, then sprite 11 will describe a circular path, otherwise the drawn shape would become an ellipse.

The speed is kept at 1 for the time being, so 360 steps will make a full circle.

Now, if you set sprite 11 to cause trails (remember, select all frames of sprite 11 and click the Trails button in the Property Inspector), and play the movie, the drawn result on stage looks like the picture (right).

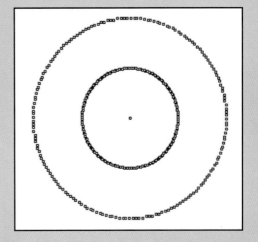

Although it appears that the second dot, sprite 11, is circling around the same center as the first dot, sprite 10, only with a different radius, sprite 11 is in fact circling around sprite 10.

Tweaking

To amend the properties of the existing Behavior, select all the frames of a sprite and work with the Behavior tab on the Property Inspector. Okay, let's try a version out. If the speed is set to 4, instead of 1, then the result looks like this picture (right):

In this picture the rotation of sprite 11 around sprite 10 is already more obvious.

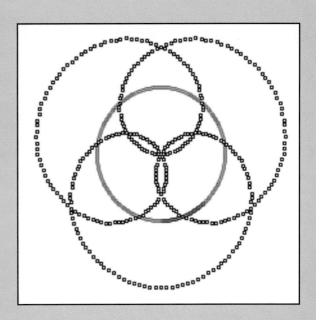

Now, for the fun of playing around with what we have created, let's add several more sprites to the score, attaching the same `circ2` behavior to all of them, but with the properties in the script set to different values.

We can firstly play with the Blend settings, to see the evolution of our piece even more clearly. Select all the sprites in the score, choose Blend from the Ink pop up menu in the Property Inspector, and then choose 30 from the percentage pop up there.

The amount of dots drawn on the circumference during one revolution can be calculated by dividing the degrees, 360, by the speed – if the speed is set to 1, one revolution will produce 360 dots, if the speed is set to 360, one revolution will produce 1 dot, if the speed is set to 90 one revolution will produce 4 dots, and so on.

There are other ways to change the values in an already assigned behavior.

One way is to doubleclick the sprite with the behavior attached in the score to select it over more than one frame. Then click the Behavior icon in the sprite toolbar of the score window, and in the Behavior Inspector doubleclick the preview of the code which again opens the pop up window and allows you to change the values.

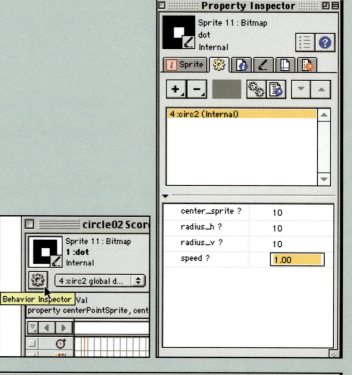

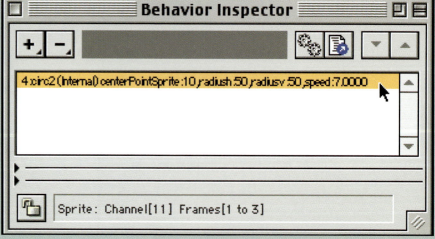

The following three examples are done by adding three additional sprites (in channel 12,13,14, additional to sprite 11) for the second movement, so that all in all four dots should be circling around sprite 10. The sprites all contain the castmember called `dot`, they are extended over 3 frames and the blend of all of them is set to 30 – don't forget to give them a trail!

Example 1
The sprites 11 / 12 / 13 / 14 are all circling around sprite 10. Both values of the radius (`radiusH` and `radiusV`) are set to 10 / 20 / 30 / 40. The speed is set to 3 / 5 / 7 / 9. (So for instance sprite 11 has a `radiusH` of 10, a `radiusV` of 10 and a `speed` of 3, and so on.)

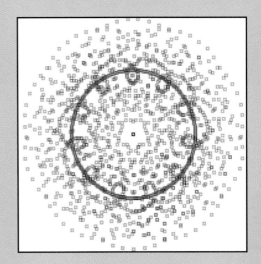

Example 2
The sprites 11 / 12 / 13 / 14 are now all circling around the previous sprite of each (11 around 10, 12 around 11, and so on.)

Both values of the radius are set to 10 for all these sprites. The speed is set to 2 for all these sprites.

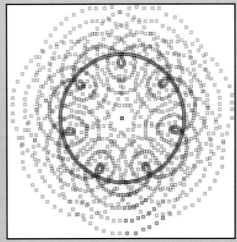

Example 3
The same values are used as in example 2, except that the speed is set to 1 for the sprites 11 / 12 / 13 / 14:

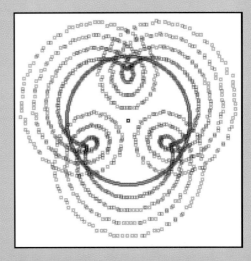

Example 4
The same values are used as in example 3, the only change here is that the value of `radiusV` is set to 20 (instead of 10) for the sprites 11 / 12 / 13 / 14.

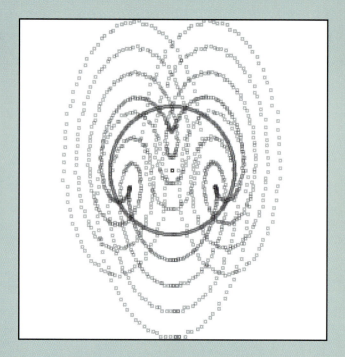

After all of these examples, it's time to start thinking about something practical. Firstly, we need to make sure this Director project really is reflecting what the drawing machine was doing.

As sprite 10 here represents the center of the white wheel, and in the original game it is not really used for drawing a curve, it should be made invisible. A short movie script is enough to ensure that the sprite is still moving around in the same way, but is not visible on the stage.

To create a new movie script click below the final cast member at the bottom of the list in the Internal Cast window. Then go to Window > Script.

Name the movie script `starter` and enter this code.

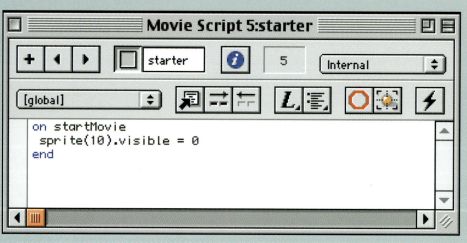

This makes sprite 10 invisible the moment the movie starts running. To prevent the initial positions of the circling sprites appearing as a drawn dot in the middle of the stage, select sprites 11, 12, 13 and 14 in the first frame of the score, and then set their horizontal (x) position to −500 in the Property Inspector, so that at the beginning of the movie they are off the stage.

Next, we want to be able to clean up the stage after the drawing has completed a full cycle. It would be desirable to include a stage-cleaning white screen, so that the movie doesn't need to be stopped, rewound and restarted over and over again when you want to see the movements of the sprites more clearly. It's a question of practicality!

To avoid too much scripting, put a white rectangle (the same size as the stage in frame 4) in one of the channels which is below the sprite used in the highest channel-number (so that it will always be shown on top).

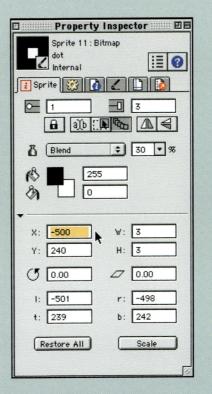

To do this open the tool palette (if it isn't already open) select the Filled Rectangle tool and set the Foreground Color to white.

The filled rectangle can be drawn directly onto the stage – from the upper left to the lower right. Then the newly created sprite (containing the new rectangle cast member) should be moved to the highest number channel (it should be only in frame 4). To be sure that the rectangle is covering the whole stage, the coordinates and the size can be typed into the fields in the Property Inspector.

Then add two markers to the score by clicking in the area below the Script Preview in the score. Put one in frame 3, naming it loop, and one in frame 4, naming it clear. (If there's not enough space to create one, you can move markers by dragging them.)

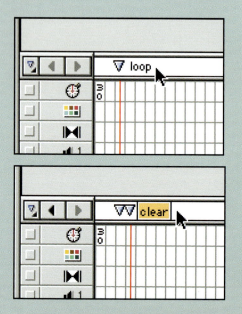

In the frame script called looper (score: Script Channel: frame 3) add the script which sends the header to the next frame if the user clicks with the mouse.

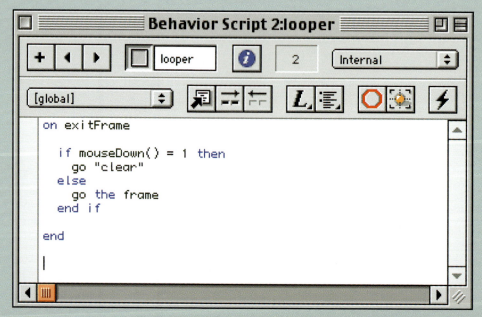

```
on exitFrame

    if mouseDown() = 1 then
        go "clear"
    else
        go the frame
    end if

end
```

Doubleclicking the Script Channel in frame 4 will open a new script window to create a new script.

It should be called `goLoop`, and simply sends the header back to frame 3 (the marker `loop`) after the screen – and all the trails of the dots – are cleared up by the big white rectangle in channel 200 (which is only in frame 4).

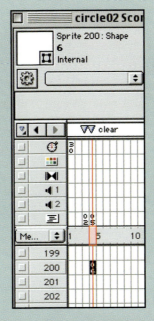

This newly created script `goLoop` should look like this:

To have the stage cleared and also allow the movement of the dots to continue – even when the trails are cleared up – every trailing sprite needs to be extended over an additional frame: frame 4.

This way, every time the user clicks with the mouse, the script carries on running and the sprites continue their movements from where they left off when the stage was cleaned up.

These examples can now be saved with various different names for further use later on. In order to continue with one version, delete all sprites apart from sprite 10 and sprite 11 and save the movie, calling it `circle02`.

Closer to the original drawings

Up to this point, we have left the value of the radius used for sprite 10 (initialized in the script called `circ` in the `on beginSprite` handler) as 50.

Also, both the directions of rotation for sprite 10 and 11 were always the same, counter clockwise, because of the plus signs in the two lines of code which give the sprites their new locations:

```
sprite(s).loch = originalH + radius * sin (degreeValue * PI/180)
sprite(s).locv = originalV + radius * cos (degreeValue * PI/180)
```

Taking a closer look at the original drawing machine we can see (or I can tell you) that if the rotation of the white wheel is counterclockwise around the center of the hole of the red base shape, then the rotation of the point where the pen is, would be clockwise around the centerpoint of the white wheel.

This means that the directions of these two movements would always be opposite to each other.

To change the direction of the movement of sprite 11 in the current movie (which is describing the rotation of the pen around the center of the white wheel), we would need to select sprite 11 and change `speed` to a negative value.

First of all, the values for `radiusH` and `radiusV` (if previously changed to some other values during experimentation) should be changed back to 50.

With a positive value of 5.00 assigned to the variable `speed`, sprite 11 rotates five times counterclockwise around the invisible sprite 10 during a full revolution of sprite 10 around the center of the stage (which represents a full circle of the white wheel in the hole of the red base shape).

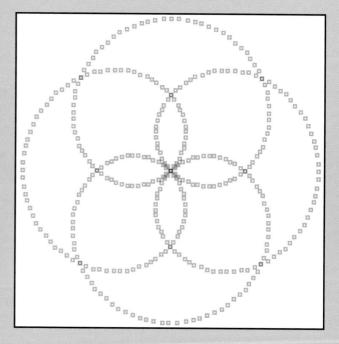

With a negative value of -5.00 assigned to the variable `speed`, sprite 11 rotates five times clockwise around the invisible sprite 10.

As the petals of the flower are still looking more round than in the original drawings with the pen, let's try out assigning another number in the negative range to the `speed` of sprite 11.

Relating this to the original drawing machine, this represents the white wheel rotating less than 360 degrees around its own centerpoint as it completes a rotation around the centerpoint of the hole in the red base shape.

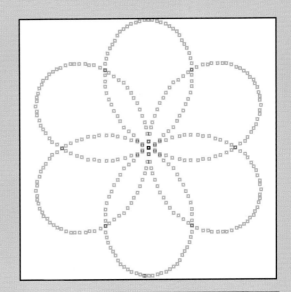

In the following example the value of -0.8 is used for the `speed of sprite 11`, while the `radiusH` and the `radiusV` values of sprite 11 are left at 50.

Now let's change some more values, so that the trails don't go through the center. To do this, we can either change the value assigned to the variable `radius` in the script `circ` (which is used for sprite 10) in the `on beginSprite` handler, or change the values of `radiusH` and `radiusV` for sprite 11.

The following examples show that what the drawings look like depends a lot on these values, `radius`, `radiusH`, `radiusV`.

The `speed` of sprite 11, used for the following examples here, is always set to -0.7.

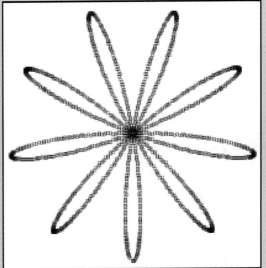

Example 1
The `radius` of sprite 10 is 50, `radiusH` and `radiusV` of sprite 11 are both set to 60.

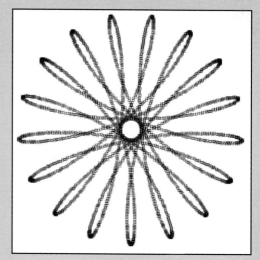

Example 2
The `radius` of sprite 10 is 50, `radiusH` and `radiusV` of sprite 11 are both set to 100.

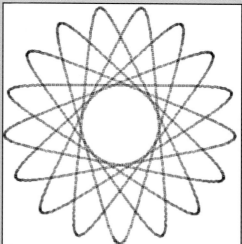

Example 3
The radius of sprite 10 is changed to 20 (in the script `circ`) `radiusH` and `radiusV` of sprite 11 are both set to 100.

Now these drawings look like the ones done with the middle-sized and small wheel. In order to make the third movement in the big wheel visible (the movement of the pen around the open shape in the white wheel), we would need to do additional coding.

But at this point I made the decision to go to step 3 of my working process, because I find it much more interesting to find out what happens if some modifications are done on the code, or some small pieces of code are added, as I don't really know in advance what results they will produce.

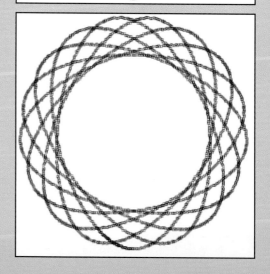

Back to tweaking

This movie should now be saved as `circle03`. There are still only 2 sprites, in channels 10 and 11. The radius of sprite 10 should be set back to 50, `radiusH` and `radiusV` of sprite 11 should be both set to 60 and the `speed` of sprite 11 should have the value -0.7 .

Sin, cos, and tan

First I will try out several changes in the script `circ2`, in the two lines which set the new location for sprite `s`. (`s` is a variable with the value of the sprite's channel number; in the case of sprite 11, s would have the value 11, in case of sprite 10 s would be 10 and so on).

My first thoughts are to run the movie several times, each time exchanging the function `sin` (sine) or the function `cos` (cosine) with each other or to the function `tan` (tangent).

There are many possibilities of different combinations of these functions in these two lines:

sin – cos was the original combination:

```
sprite(s).loch = centerH + radiusH * sin (degreeVal * speed * PI/180)
sprite(s).locv = centerV + radiusV * cos (degreeVal * speed * PI/180)
```

There can be the combinations of tan – cos:

```
sprite(s).loch = centerH + radiusH * tan (degreeVal * speed * PI/180)
sprite(s).locv = centerV + radiusV * cos (degreeVal * speed * PI/180)
```

or sin – tan:

```
sprite(s).loch = centerH + radiusH * sin (degreeVal * speed * PI/180)
sprite(s).locv = centerV + radiusV * tan (degreeVal * speed * PI/180)
```

or tan – tan:

```
sprite(s).loch = centerH + radiusH * tan (degreeVal * speed * PI/180)
sprite(s).locv = centerV + radiusV * tan (degreeVal * speed * PI/180)
```

and of course: cos – sin, cos – tan, tan– sin.

For this picture use

```
sprite(s).loch = centerH + radiusH * tan (degreeVal * speed * PI/180)
sprite(s).locv = centerV + radiusV * sin (degreeVal * speed * PI/180)
```

and save the movie as circle04.

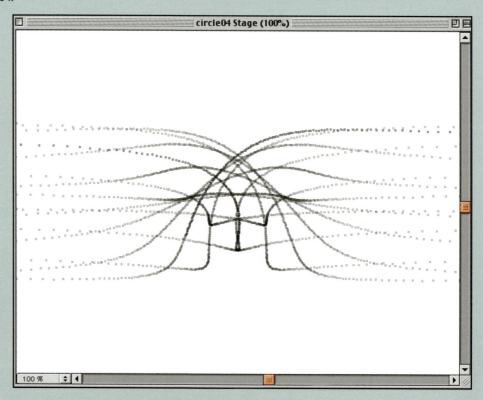

Now duplicate the sprite in channel 11 (with all its current settings) nine times into the channels 12 to 20. For a better visible result, double-click on dot in the Internal Cast window when the paint window appears, and change it to a single black pixel. At the same time set it to a color depth of 1 bit (for changing the sprites' color later on), via Modify > Transform Bitmap.

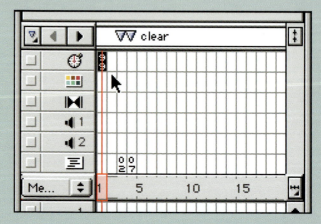

So we don't have to wait so long for a drawn result, the tempo of the movie can be increased by doubleclicking in the tempo-channel in frame 1 and moving the slider to the right to get a tempo for the current movie of 999 frames per second, the fastest setting.

Bear in mind the actual frame rate will depend on the speed of your processor!

Now – with the cast member dot changed – the drawing on the screen looks different from the one before:

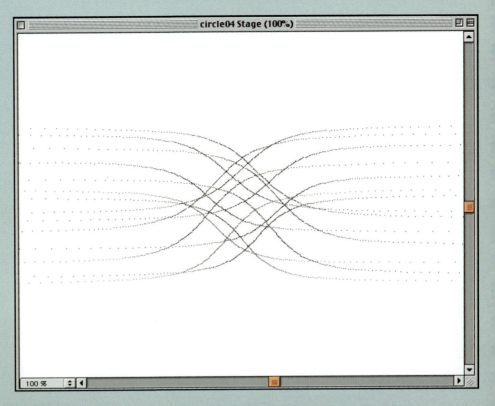

Now we'll look at including the channel number of the sprites in the code.

As each of the moving sprites are in a different channel, variable s (to which the channel number of each sprite is assigned) in the script circ2 can be changed. As this value is different for every sprite (depending on which channel it is stored in), it will give different results for each of the sprites.

The first attempt could be simply to take the channel-number (assigned to the variable s) and divide it through 100.00 (using a float number for more accurate results) and multiply the last part of the two lines in the script circ2 with the result of s/100.00:

```
sprite(s).loch = centerH + radiusH * tan (degreeVal * speed * PI/180) * s/100.00
sprite(s).locv = centerV + radiusV * sin (degreeVal * speed * PI/180) * s/100.00
```

This small change in the code produces the following result:

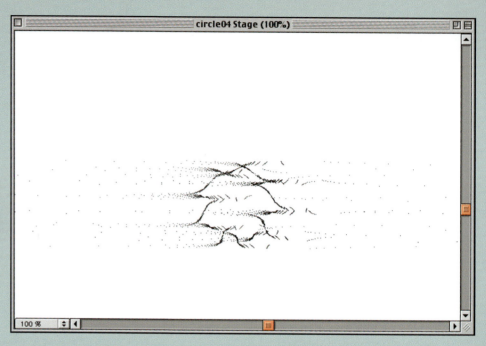

If this small part of the code (* s/100.00) is moved inside the brackets, then the result is again very different:

```
sprite(s).loch = centerH + radiusH * tan (degreeVal * speed * PI/180 * s/100.00)
sprite(s).locv = centerV + radiusV * sin (degreeVal * speed * PI/180 * s/100.00)
```

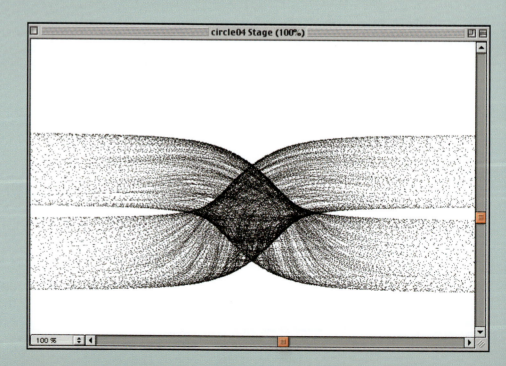

Interactivity

To allow the user some influence in the process of drawing while the movie is running, the values of the horizontal and the vertical position of the mouse (mouseH() and mouseV()) can also be included in the calculations.

First of all, as it can be good to be able to change the size of the stage later on, a little bit of code should be added in the movie script called starter to define two global variables (stH and stV) for the width and the height of the stage. This way, the movie can be resized to any size whenever necessary without having to change any fixed numbers used in the calculations.

The two new variables can be reused in the script circ2 as they are set to be global variables in the first line there too.

To include the mouse position in script circ2, we need to define another three (local) variables named dh, dv and dif.

dh gives the horizontal distance of the horizontal mouse-position, mouseH(), from the center of the stage, stH/2 while dv gives the vertical distance of the vertical mouse position, mouseV(), from the center of the stage stV/2.

dh/100.00 and dv/100.00 are included for multiplication inside the brackets in the two lines of code for the circular movement:

```
sprite(s).loch = centerH + radiusH * tan (degreeVal * speed * PI/180 * s/100.00 *
dh/100.00)
sprite(s).locv = centerV + radiusV * sin (degreeVal * speed * PI/180 * s/100.00 *
dv/100.00)
```

Movie Script 5:starter

```
global stH, stV

on startMovie

  stH = (the stageRight - the stageLeft)
  stV = (the stageBottom - the stageTop)

  sprite(10).visible = 0
end
```

The script `circ2` should now look like this:

```
╔══════════════════════ Behavior Script 4:circ2 ══════════════════════╗
║ [+] [◀] [▶]  [□] circ2                          [ⓘ]  4  [Internal ▼] ║
║ [exitFrame ▼]  [↗] [⇄] [←]  [L] [≡]  [○] [⚙]  [⚡]                    ║
║ global degreeVal, degreeValue, stH, stV                              ║
║ property centerPointSprite, radiusH, radiusV, speed                  ║
║                                                                      ║
║ on beginSprite me                                                    ║
║   degreeVal = 1                                                      ║
║ end                                                                  ║
║                                                                      ║
║ on exitFrame me                                                      ║
║   s = me.spriteNum                                                   ║
║                                                                      ║
║   dh = abs(stH/2 - mouseH())                                         ║
║   dv = abs(stV/2 - mouseV())                                         ║
║                                                                      ║
║   centerH = sprite(centerPointSprite).loch                          ║
║   centerV = sprite(centerPointSprite).locv                          ║
║                                                                      ║
║   sprite(s).loch = centerH + radiusH * tan (degreeVal * speed * PI/180 * s/100.00 * dh/100.00) ║
║   sprite(s).locv = centerV + radiusV * sin (degreeVal * speed * PI/180 * s/100.00 * dv/100.00) ║
║                                                                      ║
║   degreeVal = degreeVal + 1                                          ║
║ end                                                                  ║
║                                                                      ║
║                                                                      ║
║ on getPropertyDescriptionList me                                     ║
║   pList = [:]                                                        ║
║   pList.addProp(#centerPointSprite, [#default: 1, #format: #integer, #comment: "center_sprite ?"]) ║
║   pList.addProp(#radiusH, [#default: 50, #format: #integer, #comment: "radius_h ?"]) ║
║   pList.addProp(#radiusV, [#default: 50, #format: #integer, #comment: "radius_v ?"]) ║
║   pList.addProp(#speed, [#default: 1.00, #format: #float, #comment: "speed ?"]) ║
║   return pList                                                       ║
║ end                                                                  ║
╚══════════════════════════════════════════════════════════════════════╝
```

This is the drawn result so far, using the mouse-position of 314 pixels from the left of the stage and 234 pixels from the top of the stage – that is, more or less the center.

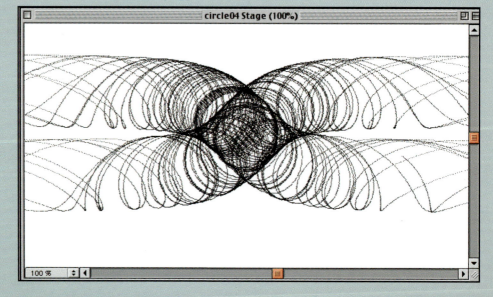

Of course the moment the mouse is moved to another position, the resulting picture changes immediately.

The little bit of code which does the multiplication with the distance of the mouse position, * `dh/100.00` and * `dv/100.00` can also be put out of the brackets – to the end of the two lines:

```
sprite(s).loch = centerH + radiusH * tan (degreeVal * speed * PI/180 * s/100.00) *
dh/100.00
sprite(s).locv = centerV + radiusV * sin (degreeVal * speed * PI/180 * s/100.00) *
dv/100.00
```

With the mouse at the exact same position as before the scripts would now produce this picture:

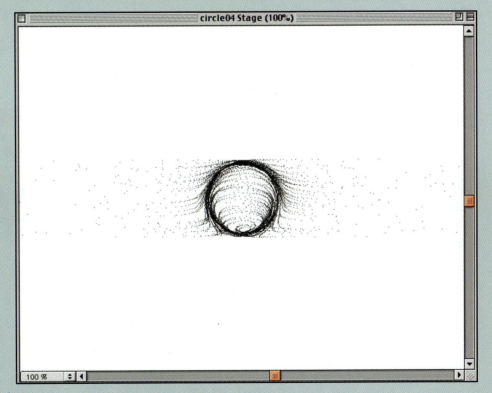

The mouse position can also be included in the script circ which is attached to sprite 10 – the center sprite that all the others are circling. If we want the mouse-position to be the center of the rotation of sprite 10 (instead of the original position of sprite 10 – the center of the stage), the values (the horizontal and the vertical position of sprite 10 when the movie starts) assigned to the two variables originalH and originalV have to be changed to the values of the actual mouse position.

The script should now look like this:

```
Behavior Script 3:circ
circ          3    Internal
exitFrame

global originalH, originalV, radius, degreeValue

on beginSprite me
  s = me.spriteNum

  originalH = mouseH()
  originalV = mouseV()

  radius = 50

  degreeValue = 1

end


on exitFrame me
  s = me.spriteNum

  originalH = mouseH()
  originalV = mouseV()

  sprite(s).loch = originalH + radius * sin (degreeValue * PI/180)
  sprite(s).locv = originalV + radius * cos (degreeValue * PI/180)

  degreeValue = degreeValue + 1

end
```

As I think the drawn results could be better than they are at the moment, I'm going to change another two lines in the script circ by replacing both functions sin and cos with tan:

```
Behavior Script 3:circ
circ          3    Internal
exitFrame

global originalH, originalV, radius, degreeValue

on beginSprite me
  s = me.spriteNum

  originalH = mouseH()
  originalV = mouseV()

  radius = 50

  degreeValue = 1

end


on exitFrame me
  s = me.spriteNum

  originalH = mouseH()
  originalV = mouseV()

  sprite(s).loch = originalH + radius * tan (degreeValue * PI/180)
  sprite(s).locv = originalV + radius * tan (degreeValue * PI/180)

  degreeValue = degreeValue + 1
end
```

If the drawn picture gets too dark too soon, check the blend of sprites 11 to 20 is set to 30 (by selecting them in the score and choosing 30% from the popup menu in the Property Inspector).

To see what the results look like when a color is assigned to half of the circling sprites, select sprites 16 to 20 in the score, and in the Property Inspector assign them the foreground color red with the RGB value #CC0000.

One of the resulting drawings could look like the picture below (the values for `radiusH` and `radiusV` for sprites 11 to 20 are set to 55):

The movie can be saved as `circles05` for trying out eventual further changes.

In conclusion

Of course one could still play with this movie endlessly: trying out various drawing results by changing / adding code, adding several different paint cast members, using more sprites in the score and so on...

But when I reached this point I decided to stop this process. I don't see the last picture here as a final result at all, because every time the movie is used for creating a picture, there are different results, depending on the mouse position. The editable Director file should rather be seen as final in the sense of the restricted drawing machine: the restrictions of the drawing machine are given because of the parameters of three different wheels, two different openings in the red base shape to rotate the wheels in, and because of having the holes in the white wheels at a fixed position.

Creating a new hole in one of the wheels would be the drawing machine equivalent further the editing of the Director file we have just completed.

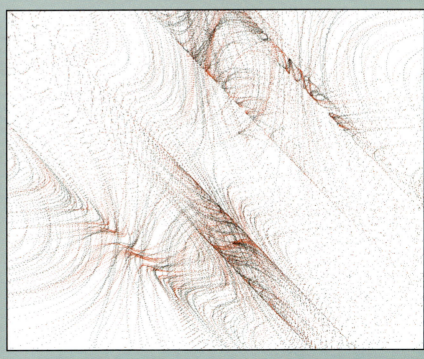

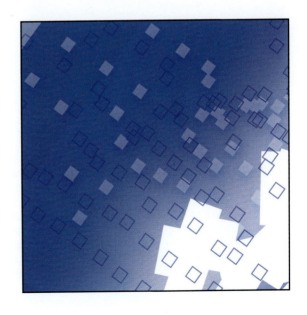

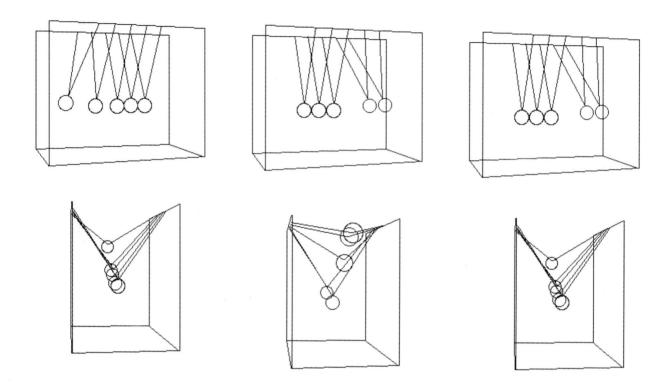

Code shapes technology into whatever form it desires. Before code, any system was fixed by its design, no matter how flexible. With code, despite its structure being fixed and defined by the system on which it is executed, a new area of creativity is opened: a definition of process rather than product.

It isn't so normal to externalize our working processes. In doing so one can put the product at risk, by making it static, but ever since the first generative ideas came about in artwork around the 1960s (take a look at the French Oulipo movement – more on that later) we have begun to realize that the opposite can also be true. Code, traditionally used to fix solidly, can equally be used to vaguely define. Code can shape itself, can shape its working environment, can adapt, modify and diversify in ways the original definition could not have predicted.

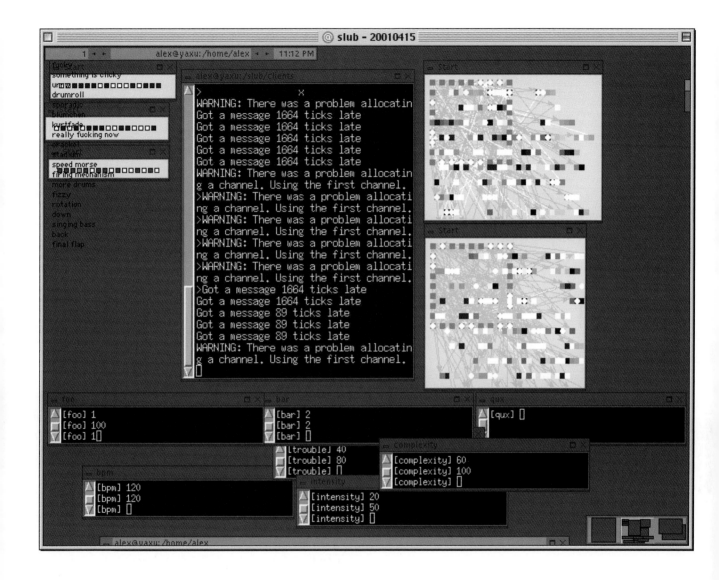

Artificial Intelligence and A-Life systems do this, using scientific models of natural systems: the neural net, the Lindenmayer system, the fractal sequence. But treating code as an expressive language (it is merely more syntactically strict that spoken language) one can see that human creativity can be codified to produce similarly dynamic results. An impulse, a desire, an emotion can be expressed using code. The code becomes an extension of the programmer, so it makes sense to treat code as an externalization of not only your own working process but of your creativity and thus your self too.

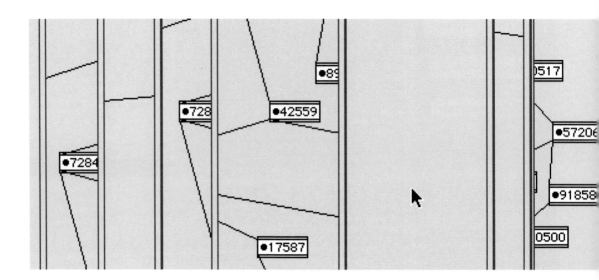

Imagine a small, eight year-old child playing with an 8-bit home computer. Uninspired by merely loading computer games into it, he starts to discover that the computer can be programmed by entering instructions into it. Imagine his delight when he sees that he can get the computer to do whatever he asks it – so long as he asks it in the right way (read Douglas Rushkoff's Children of Chaos for more ideas about "Screenagers"). How does that childhood experience change that person as they grow up?

Possessing the knowledge that everything in the digital realm can be influenced by your own hand is an immensely powerful feeling, and yet, when you think about it, obvious too. An estimated 60% of homes in the US had computers in 2001 – technology is so pervasive that we often don't perceive the distinction between digital and non-digital. Words like "chat" get used regardless of whether the conversation is taking place over a telephone, an IRC channel, or in person.

And so, for this particular eight year-old child, he didn't make any special distinction between the computer he used and his real life. When he grew up a bit (learning not to be so geeky in the process), and became interested in writing applications for other people to use, this idea grew further, into an artistic statement – one that affects the way in which people perceive both technology and art, and that makes statements about how to interact with an artwork (normally such a difficult question!).

He wrote programs that drew pictures, or made sounds, or pretended to do something that they weren't really doing. He used to go round his mate's house to play computer games on his ZX Spectrum. Unfortunately, because the ZX Spectrum loaded games off cassette tapes, the big impressive games took up to 20 minutes to load. He got bored of this quite quickly, and found it more fun to pull the audio plug out of the tape recorder quickly and put it back in, just to see if it would upset the computer. David Smith – if you're reading this, I'm so sorry. All those "R-Tape Loading Error" messages were my fault.

What happened to those computers that you could program yourself? The ZX Spectrum, BBC Micro, the Commodore 64 – their native interface was BASIC – a programming language. At some point, computers stopped providing this ability and started abstracting the user away from the coding environment. The command-line was replaced with the GUI (not necessarily a bad thing). Meanwhile, the games console completely removed the need to realize you were using a computer. The worrying thing is that there is very little incentive or opportunity these days for people to program. Where is the modern-day equivalent of Hypercard for the Macintosh? There is none. What happened to QuickBASIC? Where is the built-in rapid-application-development system in the modern operating system?

Of course – they are available. You just have to go out and find them. What a shame more eight year-old kids won't.

When my computer smiles at me, I smile back at it. It can't see me, but it's aware of my presence because I talk to it by pressing keys on its keyboard and moving its mouse around the screen. People are far more complex than that. Why are you afraid of communicating with your computer? Get it to do something new. Sometimes mine gets upset because I ask it to do something it struggles with, and then it throws a sparkling bomb at me. If you really want to argue with a computer that throws tantrums like that, install MacsBug and press Command-Power. Don't worry, I didn't understand what it was doing either, but it was fun pretending.

Think of a computer as a large block of stone, capable of being carved into any shape. You use code to fashion your technology to your own taste. In this sense, code is used to reduce the possibilities deterministically, in order to create a process. Language is also a restrictive system, although in execution spoken language produces a product: the concept.

The Oulipo, formed in France in the 1960s, played with the idea of writing by applying restrictive rules: Poems and short stories were written that obeyed strict syntactical and grammatical rules whilst still being readable. In a sense, computer code obeys the same rules, as logic must be described, whilst obeying the rules of the programming language being used.

The similarities do not end there: George Perec's "La Disparitions" (A Void) was written without using the letter E. In French, that means that there are no masculine nouns – the use of "le" is forbidden. When the book was translated into English, besides the fact that most English nouns do not have gender, it also means that there is no use of the definitive article – "the". I am reminded of the sensitive nature of compatibility across computers and how you simply cannot execute code written for a Macintosh on a Windows PC, and how in the process of translation certain elements must be not merely translated but transposed for the new environment.

an exhibition of extremely rare macos error alerts

The Finder could not start up because the version of the system software installed was too old.

To start up, use the CD or floppy disks that came with your computer. To start up from a CD, hold down the "C" key while starting up, or consult the User's Guide that came with your computer.

[**Restart**]

"a nude finder descending a staircase"

The Finder could not start up because the following system library could not be found:

InterfaceLib--CharWidt⊠™ÓêPutParamDesc

To start up, use the CD or floppy disks that came with your computer. To start up from a CD, hold down the "C" key while starting up, or consult the User's Guide that came with your computer.

[**Cancel**] [**Restart**]

"fountain"

```
pen F,'>/dev/dsp';$m='ub . . .quicksort techno. . . sl';
hile(){@d=sort{push@o,$a,$b;$a<=>$b}map{512-rand(1023)}0..
23;for(0..3){map{print F pack'C',$_;$m=~s{^(.)(.*)}{$2$1}
printf"\e[%d;%dH$1",13.5-25*($_/1024),++$f%80+1}@o}}# yaxu
```

There are other opposing metaphors for code that also apply. Code can be grown like a plant from a seed in wild new directions, each strain adopting new genetic mutations spawning new products in the process. The Open Source model, the hot topic of conversation these days, closely fits this idea that mutations in code by a wide range of authors allow a Darwinian "survival of the fittest" scheme to operate. One could say the "fittest" code is the one that proves to be the most popular.

Traditional models of genetic breeding can be applied to understand the way in which software develops. The open source GNU C compiler for Linux, called GCC, spawned an alternative product called EGCS, which competed for a while with GCC. The two pieces of software eventually recombined to form an even more powerful compiler, which is now the basis for almost all software development on most free Unix computer systems. In evolutionary terms, Darwin might have referred to this as co-evolution – the dependence of two life forms on each other.

The mechanical revolution resulted in the overwhelming urge to automate. The technical revolution empowered the individual with a dynamic tool capable of just this. While some consider technology totalitarian and fear being cast into oblivion by their own obsolescence, others forge ahead by expressing their creativity through technological tools, treating technology not as a system of control, but a system of growth. Life is given to an apparently dead technology by shaping it with one's ideals and inspirations. Code is just one physical manifestation of this – a machine-readable language that shares and communicates individual goals. This is what every enthusiastic programmer knows deep down – a computer program is an extension of yourself, and will go on living long after you disappear into oblivion.

```
open F,'>/dev/dsp';$m='ub . . .quicksort techno. . . sl';
while(){@d=sort{push@o,$a,$b;$a<=>$b}map{512-rand(1023)}0..
1023;for(0..3){map{print F pack'C',$_;$m=~s{^(.)(.*)}{$2$1}
;printf"\e[%d;%dH$1",13.5-25*($_/1024),++$f%80+1}@o}}# yaxu
```

It is with this immense sense of personal expression that I commit myself to work on code in a manner that fits my artistic endeavours. Writing Autoshop and Auto-Illustrator is just a way for me to communicate many ideas I have about issues that plague me. At the same time, I have to be mindful that these products are not just that: there are end users who will potentially pay money to use them for themselves. Writing software for the public is no mean feat – you have to be able to predict what your customers want, solve their problems and provide them with something the next application can't, but balancing that with my own artistic intentions has been one of the hardest things I've ever attempted. I don't have a specific way of solving this problem. All I can say is that when I started the project I had some idea of what I wanted to do, but no definite answers as to how I was going to achieve it (either technically and artistically). In the process of authorship, writing the software has become a way of tackling problems as they arise.

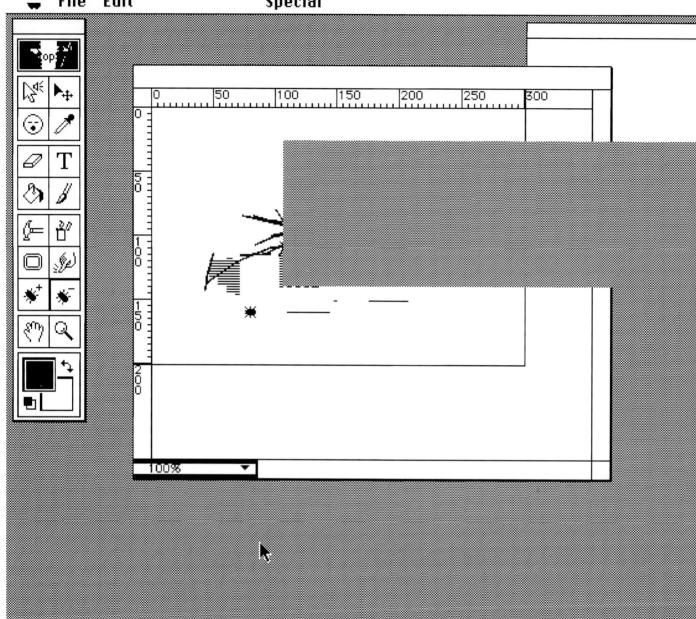

Thu 7:40:41 pm

phat pixels | **rhythm**

Pix-byte at 15,0:

630 HD

■■■■■■■

Ade Plaid Lemonad

☐ Beat out pix-bytes as drum patterns

Color: I'd prefer: ■

■ "Grey-Nice Blueish"
    HTML color #3774C6

Red: ⇦▐▐▐   ⇨
Green: ⇦   ▐▐▐   ⇨
Blue: ⇦   ▐▐▐⇨

Text tool options:

Word size: ⇦   ▐▐▐ ⇨
            Short   Long

☐ Slightly foreign

Scribbling options: [rnd]

Jerkiness: ⇦   ▐▐▐   ⇨
Wander: ⇦   ▐▐▐ ⇨
Distance: ⇦   ▐▐▐⇨
Length: ⇦   ▐▐▐ ⇨
            Less   More

☐ Enable Crayola™ compatability
☐ Watch me scribbling

Wastebasket

Auto-Illustrator is multi-faceted. It doesn't serve one purpose alone. Its existence stands as a living diary of all the things I wanted to think about. Initially, it started off as a way of thinking about automation in graphic design, but soon blossomed to include branches that splayed off at obtuse angles: how can you open source some code that is the core part of an artistic subjective opinion – surely if someone else modifies my code then it ceases to be my artwork?

I thought about ways of parodying commercial software: Adobe's legal actions against Skylarov (a Russian programmer who cracked Adobe's PDF encryption system) and Killustrator (a Linux compatible clone of Illustrator) were screaming to be parodied. How could I use Auto-Illustrator to demonstrate the ludicrous way in which profit-driven corporations were forced to protect their concepts and identities? The parody goes even deeper: How do you know what Adobe Illustrator is doing while it churns through its startup sequence? You don't. It could be doing anything. Auto-Illustrator parodies this by wasting your CPU cycles as it loads. It performs millions of calculations and throws away the results, just to make it look like it's busy. How do you know that Adobe Illustrator isn't doing the same thing? "BUY A FASTER COMPUTER!" says Intel. "YES," reply Adobe, "LOOK HOW MUCH QUICKER OUR SOFTWARE GOES!" It's easy to be cynical. It can also be fun.

Yet the driving force behind all this seemingly fraught activity is merely the desire to produce a product that others can interact with. In that sense, coding is no different to design. I take the rather abstract route of preferring to create a fluid process than a fixed product, but that is something that I see changing in traditional design arenas anyway. Computer games now deploy generative techniques to enhance game play (the Sony PlayStation 2 boot-up sequence is generative: it is different every time), live music performance is governed by the very rapid processing of large amounts of numbers in real-time (look how many people want to know how Autechre make their music: The answer is Max/MSP – a programming environment). Television and radio shows are being produced by computer programs where the exact structure of the show is unknown until it gets broadcast (The Box Music Television channel is entirely automated). These are radical times that call for radical techniques in deploying systems that do not become obsolete with time. What better medium to explore with than code?

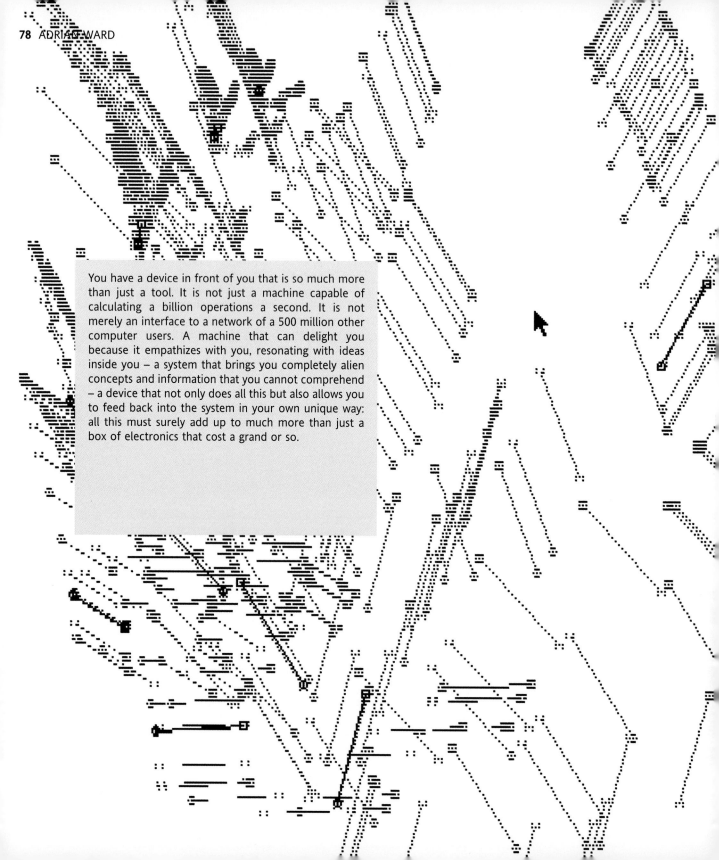

You have a device in front of you that is so much more than just a tool. It is not just a machine capable of calculating a billion operations a second. It is not merely an interface to a network of a 500 million other computer users. A machine that can delight you because it empathizes with you, resonating with ideas inside you – a system that brings you completely alien concepts and information that you cannot comprehend – a device that not only does all this but also allows you to feed back into the system in your own unique way: all this must surely add up to much more than just a box of electronics that cost a grand or so.

Seize the opportunity to use the technology to produce radical systems with roots that grow to touch others in exciting new ways. Don't let any technology fall into the well-worn ditch that so many have ended up in. The Internet has vast potential, but mostly it is used to deliver static content because business-safe practices have forced uninspired design to reign

supreme. I don't want to see yet another personalized e-commerce shopfront trying to convince me that I'm someone special. I don't need some marketing manager's must-buys emailed to me weekly in the vain hope I'll click the purchase button. I want my computer to explode with life and show me how someone else lives their life. I want my desktop to entertain and enlighten me with ideas I'd never even considered before. And I also want to buy the products I can't live without, but that's what supermarkets are for.

This idea that technology can be used as a form of personalized expression used to be purely in the domain of net.art – we saw thousands of web sites with abstract imagery trying to communicate exactly how people perceive both of and through technology. The oft-quoted http://jodi.org/ site stands as one of the earliest and most well known tributes to the way in which the basic building blocks of technology have affected the way people communicate and interact. We're now starting to see much more software art coming off from the web and onto people's desktops. Anybody who recognizes the name Netochka Nezvanova (apart from the real Dostoyevski fans) will know that the boundaries between personal expression and e-commerce business are blurring beyond recognition, (hint: try to find the sales page at http://www.m9ndfukc.org/ – please let me know if you do).

Meanwhile tools like Max (http://www.cycling74.com/) allow those who would traditionally be considered non-programmers to create code that can be shaped for use in any way. But then, what is the definition of a programmer these days? Someone who can communicate in the computer's language? An English citizen doesn't have to be able to speak English!

What I am trying to express here is that coding is not really coding. It's just a way of expressing yourself. Like learning a foreign language, there is an amount of groundwork you have to do first, but it's really not so hard. Once done, you can start to express interesting and entertaining concepts in any way you like. Code can be beautifully simple sometimes. Often the best programs are the simplest ones. This two-line BASIC program kills itself. It's really sad. It makes me cry when I see it.

```
10 PRINT "Goodbye, cruel world"
20 NEW

RUN
```

I would argue that we all have the ability to program, because we all allow this digital technology into our lives without thinking about it. We learn how to use our mobile phones, how to navigate new information structures and how to shape our systems to suit us, and our working practices. Think of the word "programmer" in the wider sense: one who provides dynamic systems for others. Use your personal creative expressions to delight others. When you shape your own systems, don't stop there – give life to others by shaping theirs through your designs. Give life! Create!

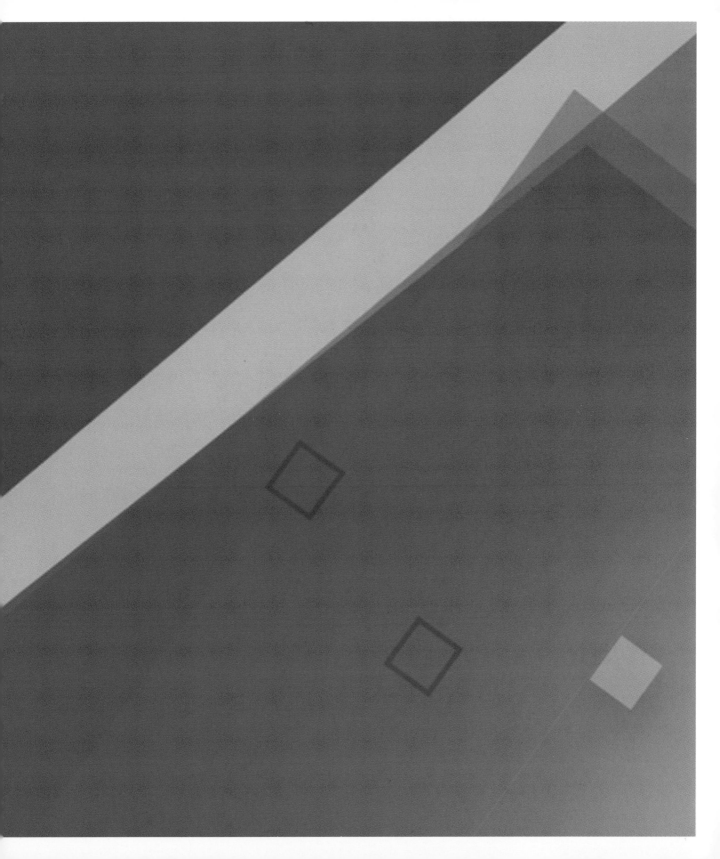

AutoMe

The mechanical revolution resulted in the overwhelming urge to automate. The technical revolution empowered the individual with a dynamic tool capable of just this. While some consider technology totalitarian (like the Government in Rod Serlings 1961 script for The Obsolete Man) and fear being cast into oblivion by their obsolescence, others forge ahead by expressing their creativity as technological tools, treating technology not as a system of control, but a system of growth. Life is given to a formally dead technology by shaping it with ones own ideals and inspirations. Code is just one physical manifestation of this — a machine-readable language that shares and communicates individual goals. This is what every enthusiastic programmer knows deep down — a computer program is an extension of yourself, and will go on living long after you disappear into oblivion.

Coding vectors

I'm not really a graphic designer. From an early age I became obsessed with writing code that did interesting things. Bored by traditional expectations of programmers and computer science, I ended up spending most of my time writing computer programs that generated something when run. I use the term *generative* loosely to describe this idea, although other people have varying definitions.

One of the things I became interested in a few years ago was the way in which graphic design and image manipulation in general were shaped by the code being used in their creation. Programs like Photoshop, Illustrator and Freehand have become increasingly advanced in this respect – often without the designer realizing that the programmers behind these tools have played a large part in the construction of the final artwork.

After writing a lot of individual programs that generated designs semi-automatically, I decided I needed to package this idea of code-as-author into a single piece of software that other people could make use of. Signwave Autoshop was the first major application that attempted to do this. A parody of Adobe Photoshop, what I was attempting to do was provide an application that actually did most of the work for you while you designed. Somewhat naively, Autoshop makes decisions, often randomly, about how your artwork should look. What you end up with is not what you intended, which is frustrating since the interface fools you into thinking you're in full control.

Since then, my attention has been turned to vector graphics – an entirely different ball game. To the end user, a vector-based application operates with similar goals to a pixel-based application. Both Photoshop and Illustrator contain a Brush tool, with which you are supposed to make brush-like marks on a canvas-like area. To the programmer, the ways in which these are achieved are vastly different.

A vector-based system works by manipulating the underlying geometry of a design. Changing a single number in a vector-based process can completely alter the entire picture, because you're directly modifying the visual properties of a construction. Doing the same in a pixel-based system often only has a minute effect, probably unnoticeable. It's like changing the dimensions of an entire building by altering one number, rather than changing a single brick to a different color.

And so with this fascination with the architectural ideals of vectors, the underlying numbers used in their creation, and the processing that a computer can apply to them, Auto-Illustrator was born. As a conceptual artwork, the program goes a long way to force the end-user into thinking about the relationship they have with their computer. As a design tool, it serves as a valuable platform for experimenting with code to produce components that can be used in designs.

Auto-Illustrator as an artwork

One of the main things I want to promote with Auto-Illustrator is the idea that authoring code is a much more effective design technique than traditional design practice would have you believe. If the truth be told, the only properly effective way to use a computer is to program it. I've always said that if you program, you can do anything. Since graphic design is now almost completely done on computers, it makes sense that designers should be exploring this realm for themselves. No longer will you, the designer, be controlled by the team of Adobe programmers!

Auto-Illustrator is also a parody of other professional applications. Where you would expect the software to behave as you've asked it, Auto-Illustrator deliberately doesn't. Part of the learning experience of using Auto-Illustrator is figuring out the quirks and foibles of the software, which are definitely not logical and are often frustrating. The intention of the software was to make something that was both productive and entertaining at the same time. Hopefully you'll enjoy figuring out how the tools work and why. This tutorial is intended to supplement that entertaining experience. You can download the latest version of it from http://www.auto-illustrator.com

Auto-Illustrator as a utility

If you can work with code, instead of against it, you can create in so many exciting new ways. Auto-Illustrator allows you to write your own plug-ins which, when installed in the Plug-Ins folder of the application, can be used in any number of different ways as you produce vector-based designs. By extending the function of the software beyond standard tools, Auto-Illustrator provides an exciting, dynamic and unique playground for experimenting with code.

This tutorial will not teach you how to program – part of the fun of learning is picking up those little tricks by yourself. (There are also a plethora of web sites out there waiting to help you.) It will explain some of the more abstract functions you can use when writing Plug-Ins for Auto-Illustrator, but you do need to be able to think in abstract terms.

To get started, you just need to know that an Auto-Illustrator plug-in is actually just a text file, with a list of instructions, one after the other. You can repeat these instructions as many times as you like, making minor modifications as you go. Rather than using the same numbers every time, you use variables – pieces of information with a name. You can change those pieces of information at any time, hence the name *variable*.

Imagine a blueprint for a building, except all the numbers have been replaced with variables, and nobody knows the values of those variables until the code has run, at which point the building is constructed! What fun! Don't be afraid to experiment. I bet R. Buckminster Fuller designed some awesome buildings before he got it right with his geodesic dome. And he didn't even have the Undo function...

Variables come in several different types. I use 'doubles' (numbers with fractional parts) and 'ints' (integers: whole numbers). When you see those keywords in my code, all I'm doing is telling Auto-Illustrator that I want to use a variable of a certain type with the specified name. You will also see me make use of what are known as arrays: these are just lists of variables. If you created an array called `friends` using the line `array friends` then you could set the name of your third best friend using `set friends(3) Steve Jobs`. Throughout this tutorial, the points that make up all the polygons created are stored in arrays called `x` and `y`, for example.

Using this tutorial

I've presented here a range of different pieces of code that, individually, produce small components that could be used in the construction of a design. My tendency is to combine these individual studies later to construct an overall design in Photoshop, although you may find some other working process easier. Don't expect to see one massive piece of code that produces a single finished design in one go. That is somewhat beyond the scope of this tutorial – and besides, if it was that easy to achieve, graphic designers everywhere would be out of a job!

Let's start with some basic concepts in Auto-Illustrator.

To begin

The pieces of code given in this tutorial are not entirely functional on their own. A plug-in requires a little bit of extra code to introduce itself to Auto-Illustrator when it gets loaded. The following piece of code should be used as the starting point for all your plug-ins. Working in a simple text editor, give your plug-in a suitable name (this is the name that appears in the Filter menu), and insert your code in between the on SimplePlugin::Launch and end lines.

Save the text file somewhere, rename it so that it has a XEO extention, and move it into the Auto-Illustrator Plug-Ins folder. Every time you do this, you'll need to restart Auto-Illustrator so that it picks up any new files you've added to the Plug-Ins folder.

```
#!xeoObject1.0

include SimplePlugin
include Tools

on SimplePlugin::Load
  set SimplePlugin::Name Type your plug-in name here
end

on SimplePlugin::Launch

  # replace this line with your code

end
```

The point

An Auto-Illustrator point lives in a 2-dimensional space. It defines a single location using an X and Y coordinate. Auto-Illustrator uses the same coordinate system as PostScript – coordinates 0,0 are at the bottom left corner of the page. This differs from other programs such as Photoshop and Flash, which place 0,0 in the top left corner.

Remember, too, that `x` and `y` are both arrays, so both these set statements are setting the first value in the arrays.

In Auto-Illustrator, we use the word 'path' to describe one or more points joined together by lines.

We use the `SimplePlugin::MakePath` handler to tell Auto-Illustrator to use those values to make a new path.

```
set x(1) 50
set y(1) 50


do SimplePlugin::MakePath
```

The line

Define another point at a different coordinate, and you can form a line between the two points. To do this we simply reference the first and second values in the arrays called `x` and `y`.

```
set x(1) 50
set y(1) 50
set x(2) 100
set y(2) 75


do SimplePlugin::MakePath
```

You'll also notice that the last point in the path (in this example, `x(2)` and `y(2)`) always has a round handle, while all the others have square handles. Auto-Illustrator does this so you can see quickly where a path ends – this is the same as in Adobe Illustrator.

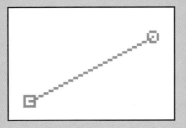

The path

Paths can have more than two points. Just set all
the coordinates before you add the do
`SimplePlugin::MakePath` handler.

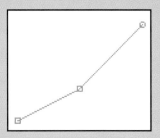

```
set x(1) 50
set y(1) 50
set x(2) 100
set y(2) 75
set x(3) 150
set y(3) 125


do SimplePlugin::MakePath
```

The vector

The direction and distance of a line between two points
is known as a vector. In mathematical terms, a vector is
the numerical difference between two points' X and Y
coordinates. Here, we make two variables called `xvector`
and `yvector`, and give them some values. Then we create
the first point in a path, `x(1)` and `y(1)`, make a second
point, `x(2)` and `y(2)`, and add our vector onto the
second point, to form a line. Note how this path, despite
being much harder to create, looks identical to a previous
path we've made. Programming is often like that.

The intention here is to demonstrate how to use variables
to store vectors, which describe basic visual properties of
vector-based shapes. We'll go on to use vectors in a more
interesting way, I promise.

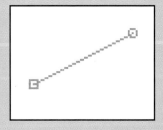

```
double xvector
double yvector

set xvector 50
set yvector 25

set x(1) 50
set y(1) 50
set x(2) [x(1)]
set y(2) [y(1)]
add x(2) [xvector]
add y(2) [yvector]


do SimplePlugin::MakePath
```

The loop

We can repeatedly execute some code using a `for..next` loop.

```
double xp          # create some "double" variables
double yp
double xvector
double yvector
int i              # and an "int" (integer) variable

set xp 50
set yp 50
set xvector 50
set yvector 25

for i 1 10 1

  set x([i]) [xp]
  set y([i]) [yp]

  add xp [xvector]
  add yp [yvector]

  mul yvector -1

next

do SimplePlugin::MakePath
```

The `for` statement has four parameters: the variable name we want to increment, the starting value, the ending value, and the number to add to the variable each time.

Thus `for i 1 10 1` will cause `i` to count 1, 2, 3, 4, 5, 6, 7, 8, 9, 10.

Rather obviously, `add` increments the first named variable by the amount given by the second variable.

`mul` works in a similar way, except it multiplies. You did notice that if you multiply a number by negative 1, you get the same number negated, didn't you?

The nest
You can use multiple `for..next` loops within each other, providing they use different variables to count with. This is called *nesting*.

```
double xp
double yp
double xvector
double yvector

set xvector 0
set yvector 50

for xp 50 450 100
 for yp 50 450 100

   set x(1) [xp]
   set y(1) [yp]
   set x(2) [xp]
   set y(2) [yp]
   add x(2) [xvector]
   add y(2) [yvector]

   do SimplePlugin::MakePath

   add xvector 2

 next
next
```

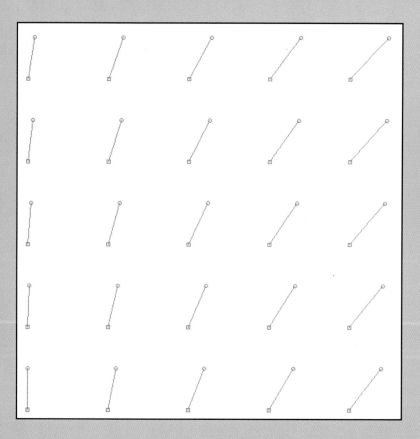

The random number

A lot of people think the word *generative* is a synonym for *random*. Although useful, the random number needs to be used carefully.

The rnd statement takes two parameters, the first is the name of the variable we want to change, the second is the maximum number that rnd is allowed to generate. rnd will return a number between 0 and the number you specify.

```
double xp
double yp
int i

for i 1 10 1

  rnd x([i]) [pagewidth]
  rnd y([i]) [pageheight]

next

do SimplePlugin::MakePath
```

The [pagewidth] and [pageheight] variables are inbuilt you can use them anywhere in your code. They contain the dimensions of the document that the plug-in is being called into.

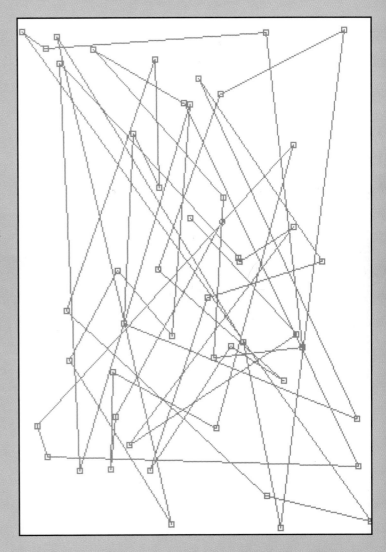

The recurring theme

Random numbers are excellent when used sparingly for recurring themes. Here, we create two random vectors, and alternate between them to create a path. We repeat this process ten times, always starting at the same point (50,50). Every time the code is run, a different comet tail will be generated.

```
double xp
double yp
array xvectors
array yvectors
int i
int j
int k

for k 1 10 1                    # repeat this for..next block 10 times

  rnd xvectors(1) 50            # create a random number between 0 and 50
  rnd yvectors(1) 50
  rnd xvectors(2) 50
  rnd yvectors(2) 50

  set xp 50
  set yp 50
  set j 1

  for i 1 10 1

    set x([i]) [xp]
    set y([i]) [yp]

    add xp [xvectors([j])]
    add yp [yvectors([j])]

    add j 1
    if [j] > 2
     set j 1

  next

  do SimplePlugin::MakePath

next
```

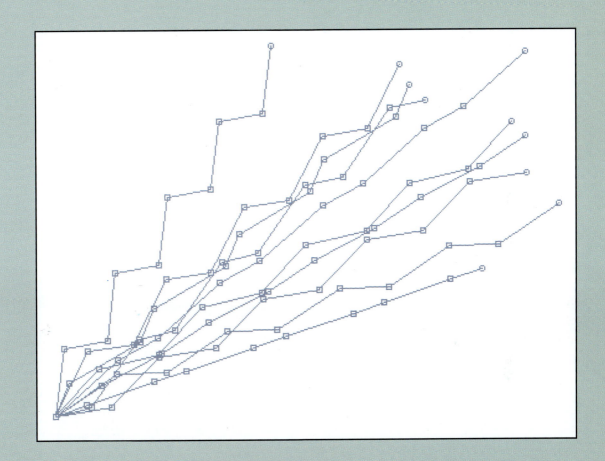

The filled shape

Rather than drawing paths as lines, you might want them to be filled. Filled paths really should be *closed* paths (where the last point in the path has the same coordinates as the first point). This is why we need an extra fifth point in our path, even though the shapes we are creating are squares.

```
double xp
double yp
int i

for xp 100 400 100
 for yp 100 400 100

  set x(1) [xp]
  set y(1) [yp]

  set x(2) [xp]
  set y(2) [yp]
  add y(2) 50

  set x(3) [xp]
  set y(3) [yp]
  add x(3) 50
  add y(3) 50

  set x(4) [xp]
  set y(4) [yp]
  add x(4) 50

  set x(5) [xp]
  set y(5) [yp]

  rnd i 100
  set filled 0
  if [i] > 50      # only execute the next line if i is greater than 50
   set filled 1

  do SimplePlugin::MakePath

 next
next
```

Here, we use a random number between 0 and 100 in the variable called i to decide if we want the path we generate to be filled or not. If i is more than 50, the shape created will be filled.

The shapes have a 50% probability of being filled. You could tweak the number in the `if` statement to change this probability.

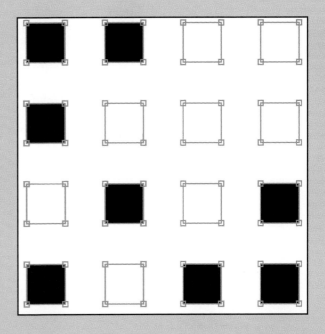

The Tool palette

It is possible to make use of Auto-Illustrator's built-in tools from within a plug-in. The Rotate tool works in a variety of ways, depending on how you have set up the Rotate Tool options, but most of the time it produces interesting effects when shapes have varying stroke weights. This code, a variation on the previous example, applies bigger stroke weights to each shape it creates. Afterwards, it asks the rotate tool to apply 50 units of rotation to the entire document. You will get very different results depending upon how your Rotate tool is configured – remember that Auto-Illustrator's tools have very vague settings anyway. It's your job to figure out what you like.

```
double xp
double yp

set weight 0

for xp 100 400 100
 for yp 100 400 100

  set x(1) [xp]
  set y(1) [yp]

  set x(2) [xp]
  set y(2) [yp]
  add y(2) 50

  set x(3) [xp]
  set y(3) [yp]
  add x(3) 50
  add y(3) 50

  set x(4) [xp]
  set y(4) [yp]
  add x(4) 50

  set x(5) [xp]
  set y(5) [yp]

  add weight 3     # add 3 to the weight of each path for every new
                   # path we create

  do SimplePlugin::MakePath

 next
next

do Tools::Rotate 50
```

More tools

Because Auto-Illustrator's tools already provide a range of instant visual effects, you often don't need to do a lot of the processing in your plug-in code. This chaotic piece of code produces the shapes you see, but the simple `Tools::Tint` call is responsible here for applying the currently selected color to all the newly generated shapes in an interesting manner. Remember that the Tint tool also has it's own vague settings. You'll need to play around with the tool to figure out what works best.

```
array xvectors
double yvector
double sy
double xp
double maxy
double maxx
int i
int j
int k
set maxx [pagewidth]
mul maxx 0.5
set maxy [pageheight]
mul maxy 0.75
set filled 1
set i 0
for k 1 5 1
  set xp [maxx]
  set j 1
  rnd yvector 100
  add yvector 50
  rnd xvectors(0) 30
  rnd xvectors(1) -30
  for sy 0 [maxy] [yvector]
    set x([j]) [xp]
    set y([j]) [sy]
    add xp [xvectors([i])]
    add i 1
    if [i] > 1
      set i 0
    add j 1
  next
  set x([j]) [xp]
  set y([j]) [sy]
  add j 1
  set x([j]) 0
  set y([j]) [sy]
```

```
  add j 1
  set x([j]) 0
  set y([j]) 0
  do SimplePlugin::MakePath
  add maxx -20
next
set maxx [pagewidth]
mul maxx 0.5
set maxy [pageheight]
mul maxy 0.5
do Tools::Tint [maxx] [maxy]
```

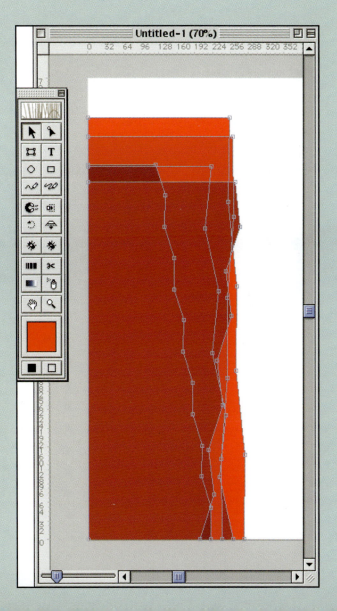

The cumulative effect

This simple piece of code (very similar to previous pieces we have seen) adds 0.5 to offset for each filled square it generates. It then offsets that square by a random amount between 0 and the value of offset. The result is that while you can be sure the first square will be in the correct position, the random displacement of each subsequent square gets higher, until the last square (whose undisplaced position is in the top right corner) is least likely to be in the correct location. The last few squares may be so displaced they are off the edge of the page.

I call this a cumulative effect, because the repercussions of its actions only become apparent after a while.

Watch out – this piece of code can take quite a while to fully run.

```
double xp
double yp
double xo
double yo
double offset

set mx 0
set my 0
set filled 1
for xp 50 500 30
 for yp 50 500 30
  add offset 0.5
  rnd xo [offset]
  rnd yo [offset]
  set x(1) [xp]
  set y(1) [yp]
  add x(1) [xo]
  add y(1) [yo]
  set x(2) [x(1)]
  set y(2) [y(1)]
  add x(2) 10
  set x(3) [x(2)]
  set y(3) [y(2)]
  add y(3) 10
  set x(4) [x(3)]
  set y(4) [y(3)]
  add x(4) -10
  do SimplePlugin::MakePath
 next
next
```

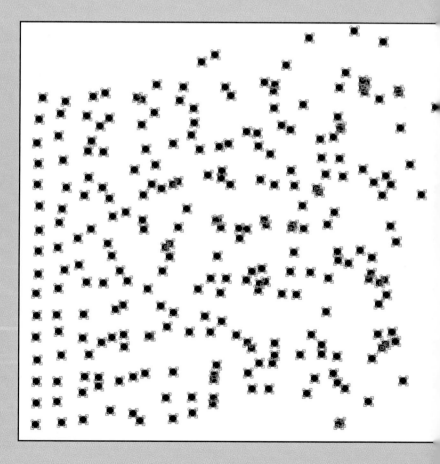

And now...

Hopefully what you've seen here hasn't been enough that you can just copy my code without trying something out for yourself. Part of the sense of exploration a programmer experiences comes from adapting someone else's work to achieve something new, hopefully learning something in the process.

You could start by changing some of the numbers these bits of code use. In doing so, watch how different numbers affect the output. You'll need to be mindful of *which* numbers you're changing, otherwise when you get something you weren't expecting you won't understand why you got it.

If you choose to play with some of the interfaces to the Auto-Illustrator tool palette (such as `Tools::Rotate`) you should be aware that the results you'll get will very much depend on the settings of those tools before your plug-in is launched, and that's a deliberately vague experience anyway (find it frustrating? That's the point). You may also be curious to know what other tools you can use. Try taking a look at the `Tools.xeo` file included in the Application Support directory – this file defines all the tools you can call from within your plug-ins. That's why you need the `include Tools` line in your code.

And remember, if you see another plug-in creating an effect you'd like to include in your own, just open the corresponding XEO file in a text editor, and try to figure out how it works. Every good programmer isn't afraid of ripping someone else's code to bits in order to find out something new.

From code to artwork

In a way, this is where my work stops. I'm more interested in the conceptual process of writing software that generates imagery, than in the creation of a fixed product. But my final piece does exemplify how users can apply these techniques in their designs.

I started off by taking a few of the tutorial pieces, tweaking their code slightly (just as you should do in your exploration) and generating them in separate documents. I also modified the settings of some of Auto-Illustrator's built-in tools, such as the rotate tool and tint tool, to enhance the results the plug-ins created. Auto-Illustrator is good for generating shapes, but I chose to use Photoshop to actually montage them together as that gave me finer control over their appearance, and how they interact with each other.

The theme of the design was *Life & Oblivion*, and I wanted to represent this theme conceptually rather than literally. Earlier I drew a metaphor between the life and death of a programmer, and the perpetual life of the programmer's creation – code. My design was supposed to be a snapshot of a moment where code was running, like a photograph of a person at a certain time. It discusses the somewhat futuristic idea that immortality can be achieved through mechanical reproduction.

Once the shapes were cut and pasted into Photoshop, simple layering techniques and transparency were applied. I used some subtle effects such as drop shadows to lift the more dynamic elements off the page. It made sense to add a small part of my text to relay exactly the idea I wanted to communicate – that code goes on living way beyond when the author falls into oblivion. I decided to construct the Auto-Me heading so that it appeared to emerge from the dynamic shapes that had been captured – the intention was to suggest that meaning can evolve from the juxtaposition of several chaotic components, a theme that echoes life. If I'd been more thorough, and had more time, perhaps I could have written an Auto-Me plug-in, too.

It is important to realize that should I create this image again, it would come out differently. This, rather than being a whimsical variation of my own working process, reflects the chaotic nature the code has taken on. You cannot control the appearance of the results with any precision – the idea that everything changes with time should be not only adopted, but embraced. Any fixed product that is the result of a generative process will inevitably be only a snapshot or by-product of the actual work. Mine is a rather simplistic definition of generative, but one which I think is important, especially as we become more comfortable with shifting media and content. Nothing is static any more. Not even a design printed with ink in the pages of a book.

Enjoy the process – work with shifting bits. Think in vectors. Forget fixtures.

Automate

The mechanical revolution resulted in the overwhelming urge to automate. The technical revolution empowered the individual with a dynamic tool capable of just this. While some consider technology totalitarian (like the Government in Rod Serlings 1961 script for The Obsolete Man) and fear being cast into oblivion by their obsolescence, others forge ahead by expressing their creativity as technological tools, treating technology not as a system of control, but a system of growth. Life is given to a formally dead technology by shaping it with ones own ideals and inspirations. Code is just one physical manifestation of this — a machine-readable language that shares and communicates individual goals. This is what every enthusiastic programmer knows deep down — a computer program is an extension of yourself, and will go on living long after you disappear into oblivion.

most of us have lost the ability to listen to our bodies.
we eat, sleep, work and rest by the clock.

sit down. relax. read this slowly.

//

the computer screen is a compositional viewfinder. it can only see so much.

everything that appears there is constructed of code. text. language.

applications. file formats. operating systems.

while we are in front of the screen they become the basis of our behavior.
we can only do what the program and the operating system allow us to do.

we come to view these structures as absolutes, as independent entities.

yet all this code, these formats and protocols and platforms,
are but one small visible aspect of a much larger structure.

a process.

a movement and flow that is completely dynamic and fluid and alive.

it is not our tools and technologies
but the rigidity of our preconceptions that limits us.

we define our systems in a rigid manner
forgetting all the while that our systems define us.

generative applications short-circuit this routine,
providing an escape from our own habitual behavior.

an escape from our own limitations
via a partial surrender of control.

the chaos and complexity and flux that permeates all of nature
is allowed to bleed into our most controlled and logical structures.

the programmers allow themselves to become programmed.

the designers allow themselves to become designed.

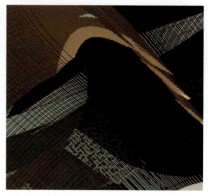

//

creativity and innovation is the transference of energy from one form to another, similar to all life processes.

the nuclear reactions of the sun, generating heat and light.
photosynthesis. digestion. respiration.

the nervous system is electrical.
sensations of touch. taste. smell. sound and vision.
all conveyed via a series of electrical impulses.

nothing between screen and mind.

//

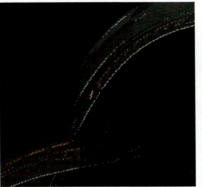
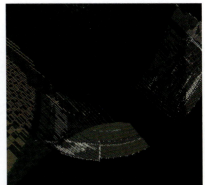

the branching of a tree. the contour of a coastline.

the whorl of a fingerprint. the flocking behavior of birds.

generative. processes giving life to other processes.

on/off. positive/negative. yin/yang. one/zero.
the interaction of the two produces everything that is.

in generative applications, code is allowed to generate further code.
some of the responsibility of decision making is ceded to the application,
which itself bears the marks of its creator, no matter how subtle.

thought gives rise to thought via thought.
a self-organizing process. order from chaos.

a chain reaction. an avalanche. a gathering storm. the eye of a hurricane.

the most powerful computer in the world,
programmed to simulate the explosion of a nuclear bomb.

//

the user of a generative application
is more like a gardener than an operator.

a gardener does not control every aspect of a plant's functionality,
does not perform the photosynthesis or the absorption of minerals from the soil.

a gardener nurtures a plant thru affecting elements of its environment.
the amount of light and water. the quality of the soil.

a plant can be made to grow in a certain manner thru trimming. grafting.
reinforcing certain processes and behaviors, discouraging others.

likewise, the output of a generative application is cultivated. guided.

there is a process that is motion.
the output is selected from moments along that continuum.

there is no final destination, no ever after.
there is only in between.

//

the image grows. the user responds. reacts.
the user grows. the image responds. reacts.

input gives rise to output. the output becomes further input.
the process perpetuates itself. alters itself.

far enough ahead, the results become unpredictable
like the weather.

a self-organizing structure emerges.

feedback loops. fractal patterns of thought and reaction.

the software, the hardware, and the user form a symbiotic relationship.

that is to say – a generative program is created in such a way
that it exhibits somewhat autonomous behavior.
it can generate imagery not foreseen by its programmer.

from a basic ruleset specified in advance,
new unpredictable forms and patterns will emerge.

these can lead to new aesthetic breakthroughs. new areas of exploration.
new influences on the programmer which will form the basis of future works.

the artist programs the application,
the application then programs the artist.

symbiosis.

//

//

in Chicago, researchers have fused the brain of a primitive lamprey eel with a
robot the size of a hockey puck, creating a living machine that tracks a
beam of light in a laboratory ring, like a miniature bull chasing a matador's red cape.

//

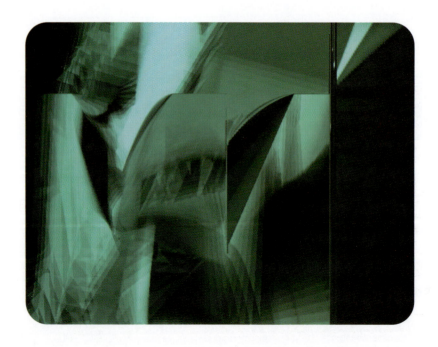

//

imagery via code.

code is a form of language.

html. perl. basic. c++. pascal. cobol. assembly.
english. french. japanese. german. spanish.

each with its own strength. weakness. perspective. flavor.
each a way of looking, a way of being.

a perspective to which we remain completely oblivious
until we step outside it for the first time via a different language
and look back upon where we once stood.

hardware and software specified by languages. blueprints. diagrams. microchip layouts.
programs. operating systems. governments. laws. social systems. religious beliefs.

each specified by, and a product of, the language that forms it.

what happens when languages are allowed to bleed into one another ?

when systems become redirected ? permeable ?

what would be the result if a system were established
that allowed the output of any program to be fed into the input of any other program
with all file formats and types being translated from one to the other in realtime ?

audio files spill into text documents, appearing as words. paragraphs. metaphors.

editing a text document triggers a series of changes in an image editing program.
filters are applied. layers are rearranged. hue and saturation are adjusted as lines are typed.

adjusting the angles and colors of a vector based image
simultaneously adjusts the attack and decay characteristics of a software synthesizer
which is playing a melody composed of midi signals
derived from the contents of an email.

what new aesthetic forms would be created ? discovered ?

how would our computing environment and habits
– and by extension, our very way of life –
alter in the presence of such a system ?

such a system would be an attempt to open our minds to possibilities
other than the ones we remember and the ones we already know we like.

we would become liberated from our presets.

//

liquid crystal displays. 3d headsets. instrument panels in automobiles.
electron microscopes. radar. sonar. infrared. x-ray.

humanity is attempting to reinvent the optic nerve so that it may see again, and the
inevitable next step will be to reinvent the creative process to free its imagination.

electricity flowing thru hardware, the monitor and the circuitry.
from the wall outlet to the computer.
from the household wiring to the wall outlet.

fed by power lines. underground cables. transformers.
turbines moved by steam from heated water. flowing water.
pulled from streams and rivers.
fed by oceans. rain.

the creative process is a part of that flow, that movement.
a translation from rain to retina.

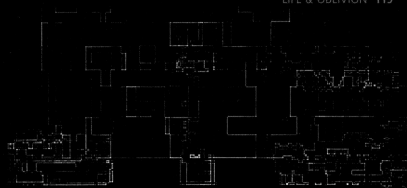

//

the internet. enabled by protocols. specifications. agreements.

code. servers. phone lines. millions of miles of wire. cable.

oceans of data in constant motion. the bitstream is alive with activity.
the slightest input causes a flurry of action and reaction.

memes. catch phrases. slang. virii. spam. pornography. financial transactions.
pop culture. history. fragments of language and thought.

oceans of mediocrity and waves of innovation.

flowing thru the air. the ground. thru silicon and neurons.

the artist taps into this flow. encapsulates it. sculpts it.

crystallizes it into visual and aural displays.

a moment in time. a flicker of light. a current of electricity.
thought patterns transmitted across the continents at the speed of light
thru networks that serve as extensions of our nervous systems.

multiplied and diffused throughout the world.

we surround ourselves with an animated webwork of complex, powerful, and unseen
forces that even the experts can't totally comprehend.

our technological environment may soon appear to be as strangely sentient
as the caves, lakes, and forests in which primitive man first glimpsed the gods.

//
an artist has the ability to arrest motion, which is life, by artificial means
and hold it fixed so that a hundred years later, when a stranger looks at it,
it moves again since it is life.

sound and image. encoded as ones and zeroes. burned into a compact disc with lasers.

translated and reanimated via electricity.

binary data becomes rich sound. vibrations in the air. reverberating in a room.

radio broadcasts. satellite communications. cellphone calls.
transmitted thru the air via various frequencies.

think of the thousands of radio stations and cellular phone calls
that are passing thru your body at this very second.

the Earth is already brighter than the Sun in terms of radio radiation - all of it man-made.

//

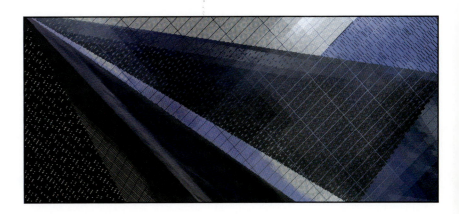

a film. a video. different frequencies of light. interacting. reflecting.

altered. edited. transferred. transformed.

light emitted from a computer screen forms an image on the retina of your eye.
photo-sensitive cells in the retina discharge electrons, triggering electro-chemical
impulses that travel down the optic nerve to the visual cortex of the brain.

there the data undergoes a complex processing that detects shapes, patterns, colors, and movements.
the brain then integrates this information into a coherent whole,
creating its own reconstruction of the external world.

finally, an image of the screen appears in your consciousness.

like data on a hard drive. transient. intangible.

merely a charge. a current. a magnetization. an orientation of particles.
a firing of neurons.

constantly edited. erased. overwritten. moved and renamed. converted.
compressed and decompressed.

remembered and forgotten.

there is a small delay between an event in the physical world and our experience of that event.
it takes the human brain about a fifth of a second to process the sensory information and construct
the corresponding picture of reality.

thus our awareness of reality is always about a fifth of a second behind physical reality.

//

constant revision. reorientation. fragmentation and defragmentation.

constant movement and flow. from one form to another.

aroma before taste. image before reality.

ideas. inspiration. designs. influences. all are in flux.

available in various forms and languages to be assimilated. recombined. remixed.

in you. thru you. the artist like everything else is a carrier. a conduit.

the artist is open to influence, yet directs the flow.

decides what to accept and what to reject. consciously and unconsciously.

translating. defragmenting. painting data upon data.

innovation is the combining of the disparate, whether consciously or unconsciously.
allowing foreign and isolated data to communicate and combine. giving rise to new forms.

transpose. translate. crossbreed.

let architecture pollinate music and music pollinate cinema.
let cinema pollinate literature and literature pollinate sculpture.

after you have seen a good movie, become a camera.

//

become a conduit. remain open. know when to act. when to reflect.
when to remain passive and when to exert control.

when to go with the flow and when to swim against the tide.

maintain opposites within you and learn how to balance them.

luck can be cultivated.

more than eight million bolts of lightning strike the earth each day.

//

we have all become jaded at the miracles that surround us.
the incomprehensible complexities thru which we communicate,
by which you are reading these words right now.

from morning till evening and on through the night
we are floating upon processes and systems that we don't understand.

meta
september 2001

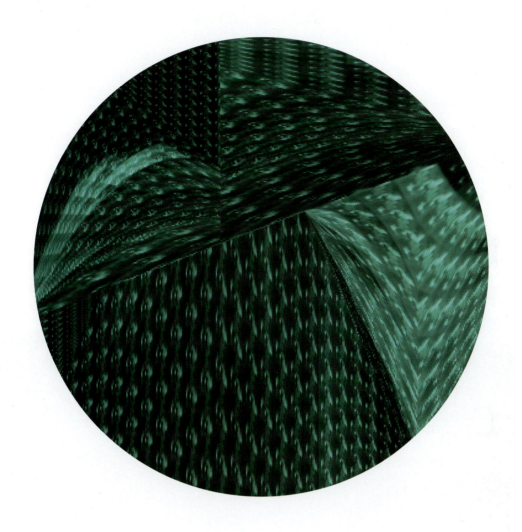

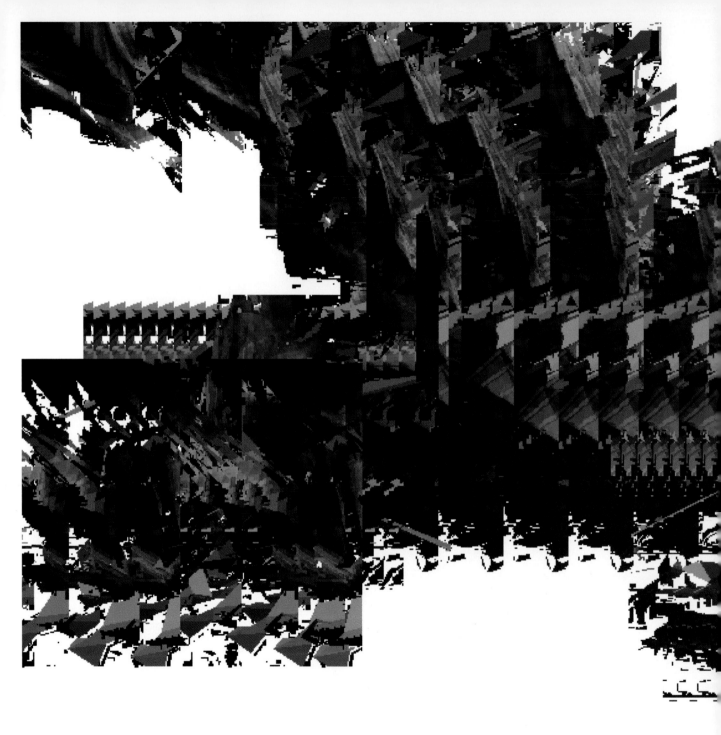

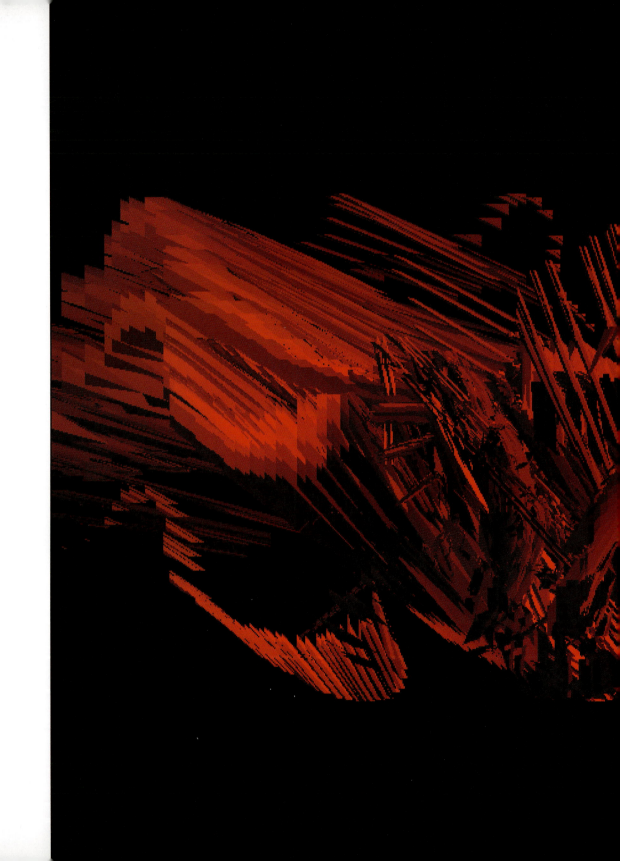

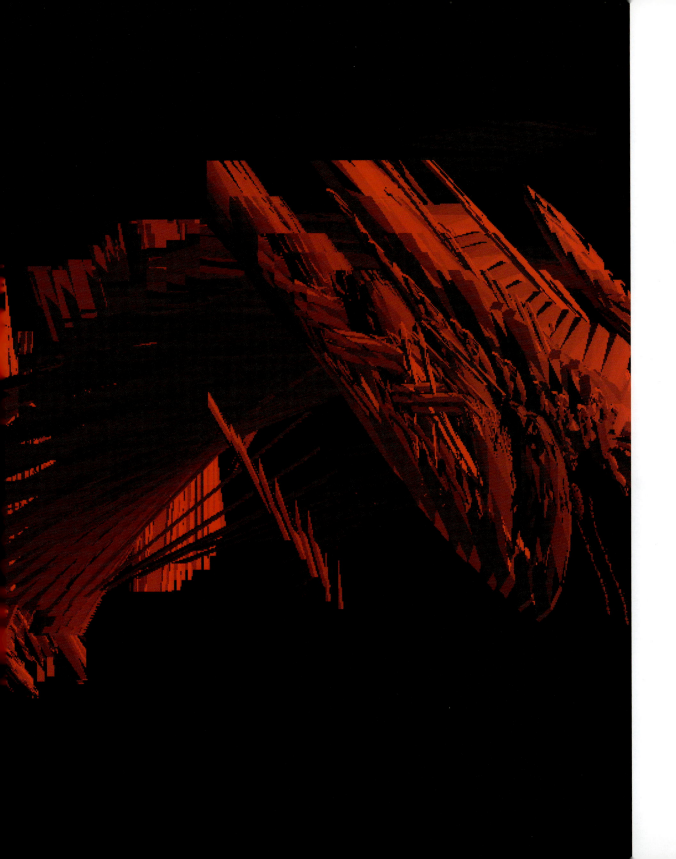

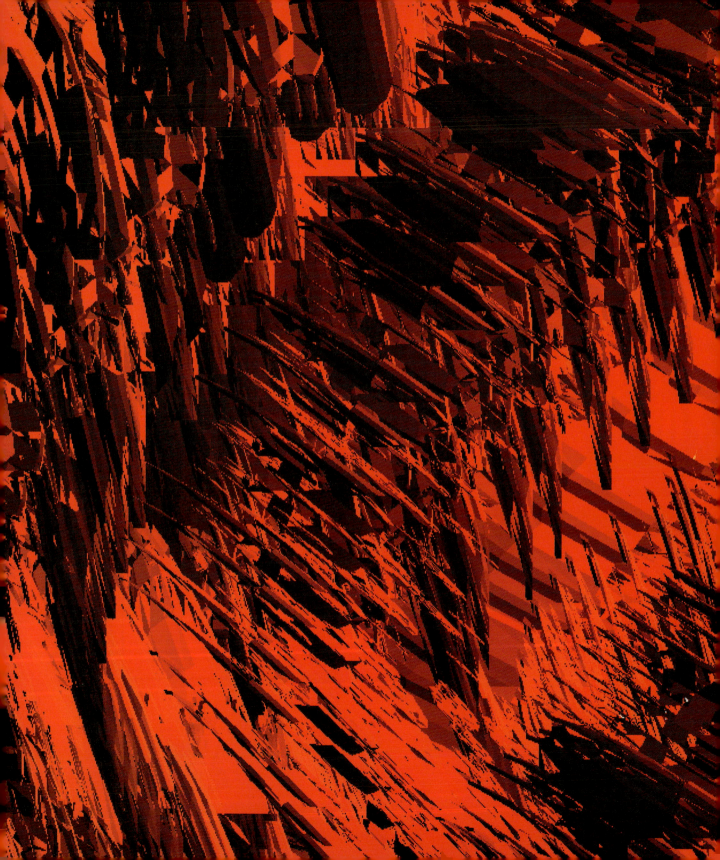

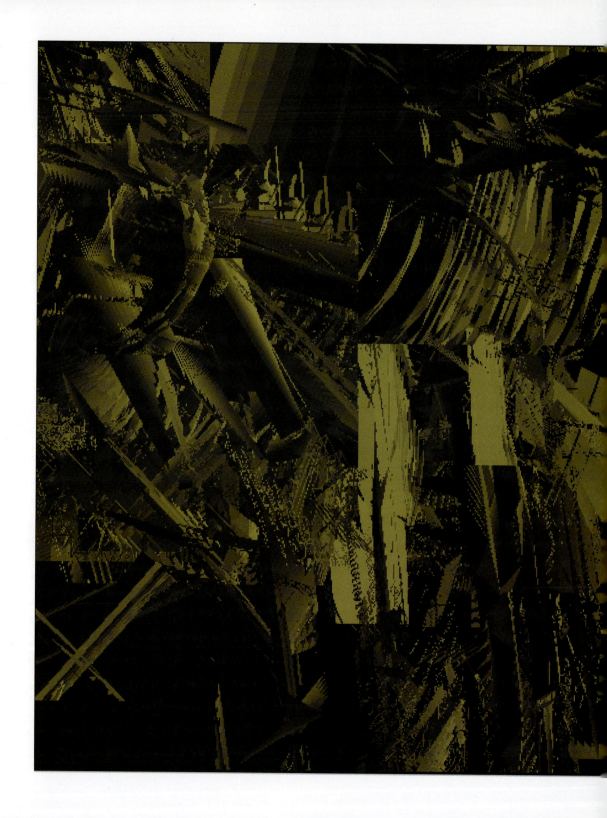

Synesthesia

Synes-thesia *also* syn-aesthe-sia *n*. 1. A condition in which one type of stimulation evokes the sensation of another, as when the hearing of a sound produces the visualization of a color. 2. The description of one kind of sense impression by using words that normally describe another.

Creative image-making with computers first appeared with the very first digital paint system, SuperPaint, in 1972. Even from this early stage, programs attempted (crudely at first but with an increasing sophistication) to recreate various traditional painting media, such as oils and watercolors. These days a wide range of tools are emulated with varying degrees of success, such as different size paintbrushes, airbrushes, pens, erasers, and so on.

A lot of programming hours and brain cells have been expended in an attempt to create digital data and processes that appear and behave exactly like a real world equivalent, the goal being to make the one indistinguishable from the other. A replica. A copy.

In the digital domain of the software and the screen, everything is rendered equal. Everything is reduced to numbers and electricity, a string of ones and zeroes – pure data. In this realm, it is just a matter of writing the code that will translate this infinitely malleable data from one form to another. A sound can just as easily be represented as an image or a text file as it can be a sound. Synesthesia.

So why make a program that allows one to paint with paint-like material? Such an experience already exists – painting.

No program will ever be able to truly emulate the wide range of subtle qualities that interact to form a real painting, the nuances of colors mixing on a palette, the tactile quality of the surface of the paint on canvas, the smell of the paint. In fact, in attempting to emulate such real world experiences one is using the computer for the exact thing that a computer is weakest at. Its strength is not the emulation of pre-existing experiences but the creation of entirely new ones.

Consider a hypothetical painting program from a new standpoint – a digital standpoint, with all different forms of media having been digitized into a common binary language. From this point of view, it is just as possible to imagine a painting program that allows one to paint with an image, such as a still photograph, or a film as it played. It would also be possible to paint with a 3D object that could be manipulated in realtime as one paints, being rotated or scaled, stretched, or any other of the transformations we currently have available to us.

Moreover, why confine the painting activity to a certain window or canvas when it could occur anywhere on the screen, directly on the desktop? Certain parts of the source imagery that is serving as the 'paint' could be made visible on the desktop while other parts could be hidden. This is similar to the 'bluescreen effect' used for digital superimposition in cinema, which involves actors and objects being filmed in front of a flat blue background. In the process only non-blue colors appear in the final shot while the blue background is replaced by a matte painting or computer animation, or any other kind of previously-prepared background.

A program is not just a static tool, but a process. As such it can do things no other tool can do – it can *use itself*. It is possible for the paint program to paint by itself (hence: generative). It is a form of autonomous behavior, although still under a certain degree of control by the user if the user wishes.

This tutorial will show you how to construct such a program on the Macintosh platform utilizing Max and Nato.0+55. The result will be a standalone functional application. (This can be downloaded at www.friendsofed.com/4x4/generative/source). It can be run and used by anyone with a mac regardless of whether they own Max or Nato.0+55, and acts as a normal, double-clickable application for manipulating film and 3D data.

Max

I should state that Max is, at the time of writing, available only for the Mac OS, so naturally this is the system I shall be using for the tutorial. However, Windows and Max OS X versions are currently under development.

The software itself is a graphics-based programming

environment, specifically designed for the manipulation of music and media applications. According to its makers at www.cycling74.com, one of its primary goals was to let users control anything with anything, through the use of event-scheduling with millisecond accuracy. Users are able to create complex mappings for incoming data, and run a large number of operations simultaneously.

Max is a complex but very approachable environment for the creation of applications and tools that do not yet exist. The flexibility and power of Max makes it uniquely suitable for the creation of custom solutions. It is ideal for those who have reached the boundaries of conventional software and are frustrated by their limitations. It is a form of programming that is of a higher level than languages such as Java or C++, and as such is much more approachable to those who have little or no programming experience, or simply dislike coding in such an abstract manner.

The nature of Max allows complex structures and interconnections to be visualized and understood more quickly, since the logical flow of the program is created and laid out in a graphical manner. To understand why this is so it will be necessary to take a look at the basics of how a program in Max is constructed.

First, the interface:

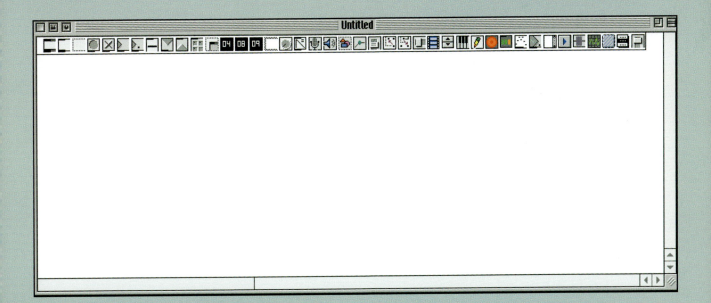

In Max, applications are developed graphically using objects (represented as boxes) that contain either text or icons. These objects appear in a palette at the top of the window. They are selected and then placed within the window and connected to form a working program, also referred to as a 'patch'.

Objects have 'inlets' at the top, which receive information from other objects, and 'outlets' at the bottom which send information to other objects. The objects are connected to one another via what is referred to as a 'patch cord'.

Objects dispatch information via their outlets in response to messages they receive via their inlets. Messages can come directly from another object or from what are referred to as a 'message box'. The message box can be triggered by other objects or by the user via a mouse click.

This basic structure is illustrated in this example patch:

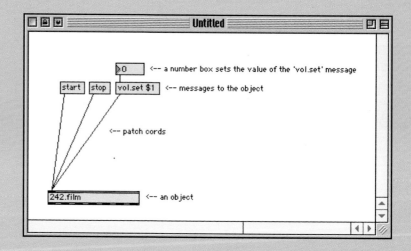

In this example, start, stop and vol.set are all messages sent to the object 242.film. When the patch is locked by clicking the small padlock button at the top-left (notice – the objects palette has disappeared) it functions as a program. The message boxes have now become buttons that send their message through their outlets in response to a mouse click. The number box is an argument that can be adjusted on the fly and passed to the vol.set message – in this case it adjusts the volume of the film.

It is interesting to note that as you construct the logic and flow of a program within Max, you are also constructing its interface simultaneously. It is somewhat like a functional flowchart.

As you might find with a quick flip to the end of this tutorial, things can become much more complex but this example illustrates the basics of how all Max patches function.

Additional software

Additional pieces of software I will be using to construct this application include Nato.0+55, which consists of over 100 objects that extend the capabilities of the Max environment. The functionality of these objects can be divided into three areas: image generation objects, image processing objects, and image display objects. Further information is available at www.eusocial.com/nato.0+55+3d/242.0000.html.

Nato.0+55 allows Max to access and manipulate all of the different media types that QuickTime supports. QuickTime is a technology developed by Apple which allows for the handling of video, sound, animation, graphics, text, music, 3D objects, and even 360-degree Virtual Reality (VR) scenes.

Among other things, Nato.0+55 acts as a conduit between Max and QuickTime. This combination (along with MSP, which is a separately-available series of objects allowing Max to handle audio) provides a uniquely suitable environment for the creation of new synesthesiac applications and experiences. This environment handles all different forms of media in one interface, making it easy to construct pathways between the two, mapping the characteristics of one media onto the surface of another.

In addition to Max and the basic distribution of Nato.0+55, to construct this application two other Max objects will be required.

The first object is 242.keyscreen. This is a third-party external object created by Luke Dubois for use with Nato0+55. It can be downloaded freely at http://music.columbia.edu/PeRColate/

The second object is autocount. It can be found in the Third Party folder of the Max distribution.

Placing objects

First, to begin constructing the application, the main objects that will be used are placed in the patch, beginning with the image generation objects.

242.film handles a wide range of media, including movies, still imagery, and QuickTime VR files. We will predominately be concerned with MOV format, though MPG and some AVI formats will also work.

242.3d reads and manipulates 3D objects (3DMF format only).

Next – the image processing objects:

242.keyscreen allows for a certain range of colors to 'show through' in an image while all others are retained and remain invisible (the previously mentioned bluescreen effect). This will be used to allow only certain elements of an image to be displayed – for example: to isolate a 3d object from its background.

Lastly, the image display objects are added.

Two small preview screens (242.ekran04) are added to view the output of 242.film and 242.3d. These screens display visual data directly in the patch window itself. They appear as two small squares connected directly to the outlets of 242.film and 242.3d.

242.ekran02 is used to display image data directly on the desktop, which will serve as the 'canvas'.

Since the desktop will serve as the background, it will be useful to be able to set its color from within the patch. 242.dkolor performs this function.

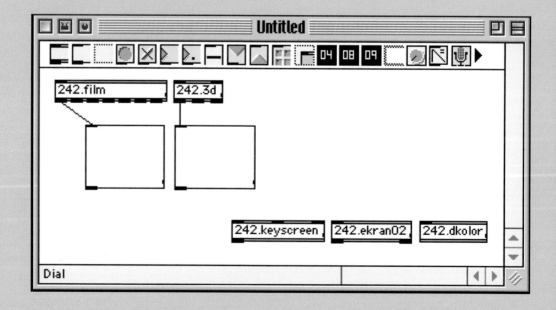

Messages for objects

Next, message boxes are added which will send commands appropriate to each object when activated.

242.film messages

242.film will receive the following messages:

read reads in a film or image. The 1 argument allows the read command to replace any other film that happens to be loaded, ensuring that only one film is loaded at a time.

start starts the film playing from the beginning.
pause pauses the film.
dispose removes the film from the application so that its imagery will no longer be processed.

The offscreen.resize message sets the resolution of the film. It has two variables: the width and the height. In order to pass more than one variable to a message, the pack object is needed.

The pack object combines a series of numbers into a list that can be passed to a message. In this case the first number box will set the width (corresponding to the first variable of the message) and the second number box will set the height (second variable).

Because the pack object only sends out its list in response to a number in its first inlet, a button (the small box containing a circle) is used to connect the second number box to the first inlet. The button will send a 'bang' (a basic Max signal that tells an object or a message to perform its function, acting as a trigger) whenever the second number box is changed, thus ensuring that the resolution is changed whenever either value is altered. This basic setup will be used whenever it is desirable for pack to send out its list when any variable is changed, as opposed to only the first one.

The rate message sets the playback rate of the film. The first variable ($1) controls the rate and is set by the number box, while the second variable (20) indicates the default rate of the film. Therefore, a rate of 10 plays the movie at half speed, a rate of 20 plays the movie back at normal speed, and a rate of 40 plays the movie back at double speed, while negative values play the film in reverse.

It is also worth noting that 242.film can read in still imagery as well. If this is the case obviously the start, pause, and rate commands will have no effect.

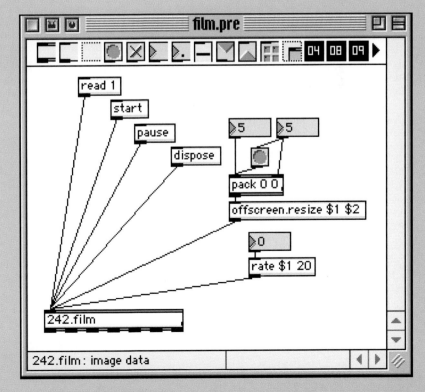

242.3d messages

242.3d will be receiving a wide range of messages:

Firstly, the object itself is created with the 320 240 argument. This sets the default resolution of the object at 320 x 240. This can be adjusted at any time however by the offscreen resize message. The same offscreen.resize message that was created for use with the 242.film object will be used to adjust 242.3d as well.

The read and dispose messages function the same as with 242.film, only with 3D objects.

bgcolor sets the background color of the 3D object. The first argument sets the alpha value. This value will not be useful for the purposes of this application so it is set to 0. The next three arguments specify the red, green, and blue values respectively. As before, the pack object and button is used to send all the variables to the message (this structure is used for all of the messages shown here that receive multiple variables, but for the sake of clarity they have been omitted from the example image over the page).

fillstyle allows the object to be displayed as solid, a wireframe, or a set of points.

rotate sets the angle and amount of rotation for each axis (x, y, and z). In order for the object to rotate smoothly this message will need to be triggered repeatedly at a high rate. The 'metro' object is used to accomplish this. The 'metro' object outputs bangs at a set interval. This interval is set via its argument and represents a number of milliseconds. In this case it is set at 80 milliseconds, however this value can be changed via the number box

(3D rotate rate). The metro object is activated by a toggle (the small box containing an x connected to its first inlet).

So if the values of the three number boxes providing arguments to the rotate message are 1, 2, and 3 respectively, and the metro toggle is checked, the 3D object would be rotated by 1 degree about its x axis, 2 degrees about its y axis, and 3 degrees about its z axis every 80 milliseconds. This perhaps sounds more complex than it actually is. The behavior will become much more apparent when actually operating the application and seeing the results of adjusting the variables in realtime.

The scale message sets the objects scale along each axis. The fourth number box controls the values of the first three in case it is desired to increase or decrease the size of the 3D object proportionally (set the x, y, and z scale values simultaneously to the same value).

The quaternion message performs a more complex rotating and twisting of the object. Try it out, and have a play with its values to see the different effects you can achieve. Sometimes it is better to go hands on than using the cerebral approach.

The point, direct, and ambient message-sets control the properties of the three different light sources that illuminate the 3D object. The initial variable turns the light sources on (1) and off (0). The next sets the brightness of the light source. The last set determines the red, green, and blue values respectively of the light sources' color.

Finally, the `direct.direction` message controls the direction the direct light is pointing in. Again, the effects of this will be more apparent when using the application.

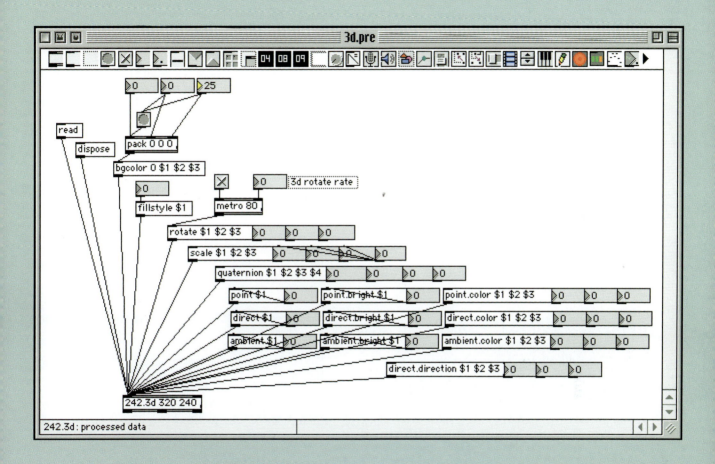

242.ekran02 messages

242.ekran02 is the display object responsible for actually drawing the film and 3D data on the desktop. It receives the following messages:

copymode 36 renders the background of the incoming imagery transparent, allowing it to be drawn directly on the desktop without the frame around it being visible. As is visible in this example, the copymode 36 inlet is connected to a loadbang object. loadbang is a simple but useful object that sends out a bang whenever a patch is opened. It can be used to initialize values. In this case, the copymode 36 message will be triggered immediately upon activation of the patch and remain active.

The loadbang object also triggers the max hidemenubar message. This is a special message that communicates directly to the Max application itself and tells it to hide the Macintosh menu bar at the top of the screen since it will not be needed while this program is running.

The coords.set message sets the x and y coordinates of the imagery on the desktop. As previously mentioned,the location of this imagery will be set via mouse movement. In order to accomplish this an additional object is needed.

The mousestate object continually reports the x and y coordinates of the mouse through its second and third outlets. These outlets are connected to the coords.set message to set the location of ekran02 on the desktop. Prior to this the x and y values will be subtracted by 160 and 120 respectively in order to center the imagery behind the cursor (as opposed to the cursor determining the location of the top left corner of the imagery, as is normally the case). Note that this assumes the size of the imagery is 320 x 240. If larger or smaller imagery is to be used then these values will have to be adjusted.

Adding key commands

It will be useful to create a series of key commands to control some basic functions of this program to allow for more intuitive operation. The key object is added in order to receive input directly from the keyboard. Its left outlet reports the ascii value of the key that is pressed. This will be used to construct the key commands along with the select object.

The select object monitors all input it receives in its inlets until it receives a value that matches its internal value, at which time it sends out a bang. Its internal value is the value that follows its name in the object box. For example: 'select 12' will do nothing until it receives the number 12, at which time it will send a bang through its outlet.

This can be used to trigger additional messages. In this case the following keys will be used to activate messages that perform various functions as follows:

The 'q' key (select 113) will be used to switch mouse tracking on and off (in case it is desired to freeze the imagery in a certain location of the screen while doing other things with the mouse.)

The 'e' key (select 101) will be used to switch the imagery on and off.

The 'c' key (select 99) will be used to clear the entire screen.

The spacebar (select 114) will be used to start and stop the film and/or the rotation of the 3D object.

The gray squares containing the three small circles and an arrow is a Max object called gswitch. A gswitch is used to direct input in one of two possible directions. A gswitch directs the input it receives in its right inlet to the outlet indicated by the arrow. This arrow is switched from one outlet to another in response to a bang in its left inlet.

As can be seen in this example, the gswitch object is used in conjunction with the key and select objects to direct the selected keyboard input alternatively between two different options, like a toggle. Repeatedly pressing the 'q' key will switch between poll and nopoll modes, repeatedly pressing the 'e' key will activate and then deactivate the imagery, and so forth.

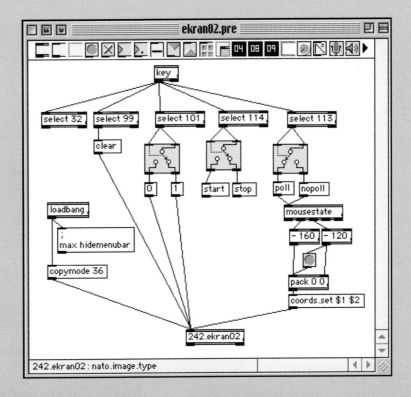

242.dkolor will receive only one message: `color`.

The `color` message receives three arguments which correspond to the red, green, and blue values of the color that the desktop is to be set to. A multislider object is used to provide these values.

The multislider functions in a similar fashion to a multiband graphic equalizer. One clicks within the multislider and drags up or down to set the values for each slider. The number of sliders and the range they output can be set by selecting the object within the patch and pressing cmd-i on the keyboard. A menu will appear in which the various options can be set. In this case three bands are used to supply their values to the color message. One can adjust the multislider settings and observe the desktop color change in realtime.

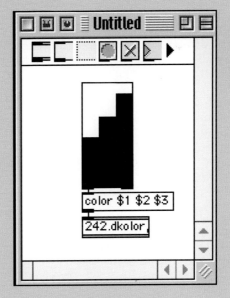

242.keyscreen data

All that remains now is to supply the necessary data to 242.keyscreen. Two 242.keyscreen objects will be utilized: one for 242.film and one for 242.3d.

As previously mentioned, the keyscreen objects will be responsible for isolating certain film elements or 3D objects from their backgrounds. In order to do this a color must be specified as the key. The key color is the color that will show through and appear against the desktop. A fuzziness value can be set that will determine how strict or liberal 242.keyscreen should be in interpreting these RGB values. For example, a low fuzzy value will allow only the specified color to show through. A higher fuzzy value will allow a higher range of colors to become visible.

Each 242.keyscreen will need the following input supplied to it:

The image data to key.
The RGB values of the color that will be keyed.
The 'fuzziness' value.

The image data to be keyed is obtained directly from 242.film and 242.3d. Their outlets are connected to their respective 242.keyscreen inlets (not shown in this example).

The RGB values to be keyed could be supplied via typical number boxes, but this is slow and unintuitive. Instead, these values will be obtained from the small preview screens (242.ekran04) that were created previously for displaying the direct output of 242.film and 242.3d.

When the mouse is clicked or dragged within the 242.ekran04 window, the RGB values at the cursor location are sent out of its first outlet. This data is passed through 242.rgblx, which scales these numbers into a value suitable for 242.keyscreen. The RGB message is then prepended to these values (utilizing the prepend object) which gives the command to set the key color.

Now in order to set the key color for the film, one can click on a color in the small preview window. The same is true for the 3D preview. The key color for each image source can now be set independently with one mouse click.

The RGB 'fuzziness' value mentioned earlier will be set with a simple number box.

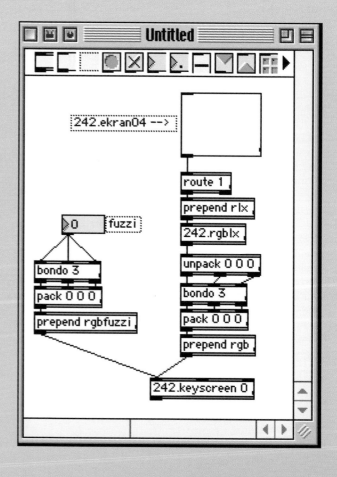

Rounding off

The final part of the application to create is the 'autopilot' mode, which will allow the application to paint on its own – with or without user input. To enable this we will need to feed random numbers to those parameters we want to operate on their own. The parameters we will put under random control will be the location of the imagery on the desktop (the x and y coordinates of 242.ekran02), and the rotation and scale settings of 242.3d.

The 3D rotation and scale settings will simply be controlled by the random object. The random object outputs a random number that is between 0 and one less than its range every time it receives a bang. The range of the random object is specified when the object is created. For example, random 20 will output a random number between 0 and 19 every time it receives a bang. The range can also be specified on the fly via a number box supplying a value to the random objects right inlet.

In this case we will use three random 10 objects to supply values to the three 3D rotate variables (x, y, and z axes) and three random 20 objects to supply values to the three 3D scale variables (again, the x, y, and z axes). These are useful initial values but in the event that the user wishes to set their own ranges we will provide a number box connected to each random object for this purpose. The functionality of these number boxes is identified by the '3D rotate rand range' and the '3D scale rand range' comments.

The bangs that these random objects require will come from a metro object with an initial value of 1000, thus outputting a bang every second (the 1000 represents 1000 milliseconds). This metro object will be activated via a toggle and a number box will be used to alter its rate (3d rand rate).

The autocount object will be used to supply random values to control the x and y coordinates of the imagery on the screen. The autocount object provides a much finer degree of control over its functionality than the random object does. One can set high and low values between which a random number must fall, as well as select from among six different modes for number generation: up, down, updown, downup, oscillate, and random.

The autocount object is initialized with various values that set the type of count, minimum and maximum values to output, the step value (amount of numbers to skip when counting sequentially), as well as the speed with which the values will be output. For example: the autocount that will drive the x coordinates of the imagery on the screen will be intialized as follows: autocount random 0 0 1024 1 1000

random is the method of number generation.
The first 0 represents the starting value.
The second 0 represents the minimum value.
The 1024 represents the maximum value (it is set to this value assuming a 1024 x 768 resolution display).
The 1 represents the step value.
The 1000 represents the number of milliseconds between number generation.

The autocount that will supply the y coordinate values is set up the same as this one, except 450 is used for the maximum value (again assuming a 1024 x 768 resolution and allowing some space at the bottom of the screen for the application itself).

All of these values can be adjusted on the fly. Four number boxes are connected to the various inlets of each autocount to change the minimum, maximum, step, and rate values if the user wishes.

All of these metro and autocount objects will be triggered by pressing 'r' key on the keyboard. As with the previously constructed key commands, the output of key object is connected to a select object (114 is used as the value of the object, being the ascii value of the r key).

The select object will trigger a gswitch object that will toggle the autocount and metro objects. The outlet of the metro objects will be connected to the various 3D scale and rotation parameters they are meant to control. The outlet of the autocount objects will be connected to the '–160' and '–120' objects that were previously created to receive the x and y coordinate values from the mousestate object. These objects are still performing the same role as before, only now they are receiving their values from a random number generator autocount in addition to the users cursor position (mousestate). Both options will be active at once, so if the user was to move the cursor while the random numbers from auto-count were being sent, an interesting battle would take place between the application and the user in determining the location of the imagery on the screen.

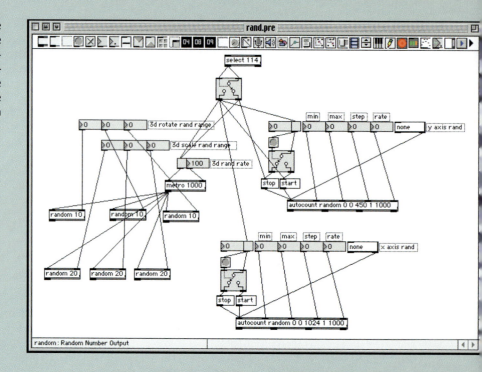

All of the objects and connections are now complete. The
arrangement of the patch is cleaned up and organized to
provide a clear and compact layout for the user interface.

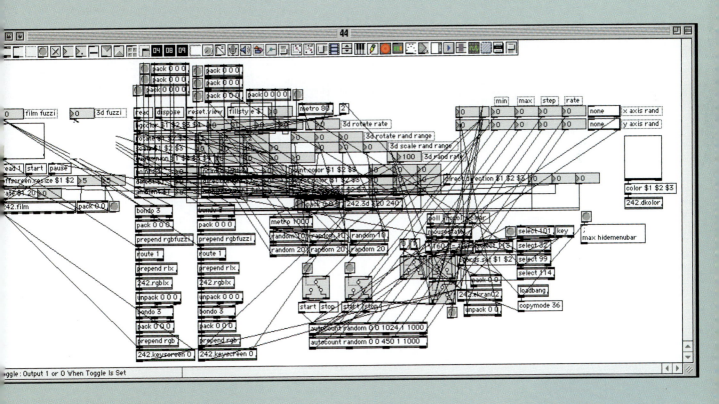

The numerous patch cords and objects unimportant to
the user interface are hidden to eliminate the clutter. A
hidden object is an object that becomes invisible once the
patch is locked and run. Any object or patch cord can be
hidden in Max by simply selecting it and pressing cmd-k
on the keyboard.

The application is now complete.

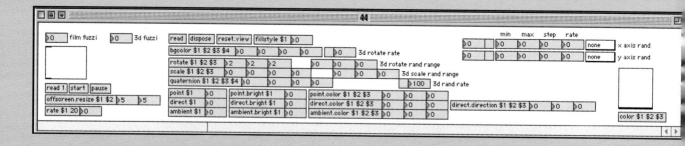

Load film and 3D data.
Set it in motion.
Set the key color & fuzzy levels.
Set the desktop color.
Set the copymode.
Experiment.

I. Designing with Code: One Artist's Journey

Most art schools today teach classes in Digital Art, which to them means How to Use Adobe Photoshop. Although such courses often claim to explore the possibilities of a new medium, they generally explore little more than the possibilities that somebody else (namely, Adobe) has found convenient to package in a piece of commercial software. The fact is that computers are capable of a far greater number of things than any specific piece of software might lead us to believe. In the short essay I present here, it is my intention to encourage visual artists to understand and work beyond the limitations imposed on them by their software tools. Whereas the other books in this series may have focused on the tricks that allow one to get the most out of Photoshop, I'd like to offer a glimpse of what can be achieved when artists step away from Photoshop altogether, and make their own software tools – with code.

Popular tools like Photoshop and Director have been both a great boon and a great hindrance to the development of interactive media art. On the one hand, they have democratized the production of digital media: today, anyone with a computer can publish and distribute an image or text on the World Wide Web. On the other hand, these tools homogenize the process and products of interactive art.

With identical options to choose from, everyone's art begins to look and taste the same.

I believe individual artists should *dictate* the possibilities of their chosen media, and not leave it to the Adobes and Macromedias of the marketplace. The notion of artists creating their own tools is as old as art itself. For centuries, artists ground their own pigments, plucked pig hairs to make their own brushes, and primed their own canvases with glue made from boiled rabbits. Instead of distracting artists from their true purpose, these crafts actually tightened artists' connections to their materials and process.

The revolution in software tools over the past decade, by contrast, has been a disaster for the intimate relationship between practice and practitioner. Our tools, created by anonymous engineers for nobody in particular, are mass-produced, mass-distributed, one-size-fits-all. And all too often, we have no idea how we might make such a tool for ourselves, even if we wanted to. In this essay, I hope to reclaim tool-making for the artists. The territory has largely shifted from paint to code: so that is where we must go.

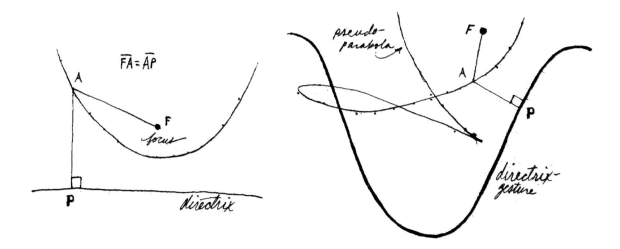

Picking up code

Of course, it's one thing to declare the necessity of programming skills in the field of digital art, and quite another to actually acquire and develop such skills. So I thought it might be helpful or encouraging to share my own story about how I learned to program the software artworks I now make. I certainly wasn't born a programmer. In fact, my background before 1994 was almost entirely in fine arts and music composition. I wasn't even especially eager to learn programming. Computer Science was so poorly taught when I was an undergraduate that I quickly lost interest. The professors would spend an entire week treating the matter of "floating-point roundoff accumulation errors," and I couldn't have cared less. It didn't help that most of the Computer Science students were already experienced programmers.

Trained as I was in visual arts and music, I was seeking a Studio Art course in Computer Science. I daydreamed about a hypothetical course of study in which I would be permitted to assign myself my own problems. Then I'd learn as I went, learning how to solve problems because they were meaningful to *me*. I wasn't lucky enough to find such a course at the time, and so I graduated college with pretty much the same skills I entered with.

When I finished undergraduate school I got my first job, working as a graphic designer in a Silicon Valley research company. I was responsible for making thousands of Macintosh icons for an experimental software system called *Media Streams*. These icons comprised the hieroglyphic vocabulary of a comprehensive visual language for video annotation. In theory I had to create an icon for anything that might ever occur in a video or film. I ended up making something close to 8,000 icons.

After a few years I started to have dreams that took place in a 32-by-32-pixel universe. People often talk about whether we dream in color or black and white – I can say for certain that I had at least a few dreams in the 8-bit Macintosh system palette. As my enthusiasm for pixel-pushing dwindled, I found new sources of stimulation in the culture of software development all around me. It was 1994, some friends and mentors had freshly introduced me to the concept of Interactive Art, and I wanted more than anything else to understand this new form of expression, albeit at a basic level.

Around that time I was reading Wassily Kandinsky's *Point and Line to Plane* (1926), Gyorgy Kepes' *Language of Vision* (1944), and Paul Klee's *Pedagogical Sketchbook* (1923). All three of these books are masterpieces of design pedagogy by some of the foremost thinkers of the Bauhaus movement. In their teachings, Kandinsky, Kepes and Klee sought to encourage a rigorous study of what they considered to be the basic formal elements of visual communication: point, line, plane, texture, color, rhythm, balance, and so forth. Only by precisely investigating these basic building materials of graphic communication – in isolation and then in restricted combinations – could an art student eventually hope to successfully create more complex compositions. It seemed logical to me that a similar approach could be applied to the study and creation of interactive systems.

I wanted to understand what the formal elements of interaction *were*. The designers I knew all used and recommended Macromedia Director, and so I decided to start there.

Director

The first thing I noticed about using Director was that it was incredibly easy to trigger QuickTime videos, stereo sound clips, and scene transitions – but difficult, say, to draw a simple line. Macromedia finally fixed this a year or two ago, but in 1994, animating an arbitrary line in Director required about a page of rather peculiar code to switch between two different cast members – it was needlessly awful. If that wasn't enough, Director made it impossible to rotate a graphical element! Instead, it forced all the visual elements into static orientations, like soldiers locked into upright positions. What's more, Director limited the number of simultaneously manipulable elements to 160. These seemed like basic injustices to me.

What is the proper response to such constraints? I knew one particularly committed and talented young designer, who, when he wished to rotate a graphical element in Director, would prepare hundreds of rotated bitmaps beforehand in another tool like AfterEffects. I recall one occasion when he wanted to control two parameters of a shape at the same time – rotation and color – and the poor fellow ended up pre-rendering a matrix of 10,000 images. He wasn't making

fancy graphics, either – just squares and triangles. There was *no* reason a computer couldn't render such a simple shape. The results of his labor were stunning – nobody had *ever seen* Director look like that before – but I couldn't avoid the feeling that my colleague was being bullied by the tool he was supposed to be controlling.

Director's structure positively offended me, not only because of the fundamental things it prevented me from doing, but also because of what it suggested I *ought* to be doing instead – making dithery scene transitions between QuickTime videos. This wasn't what I perceived interactive multimedia to be. By 1996 I had encountered more limitations than I could tolerate. I wanted to be able to control a thousand rotating squares, and I didn't feel like waiting out the four years (and three versions of software) that it would take before Macromedia eventually turned its attention to my needs.

With a great deal of anxiety I came to the slow realization that all of the things I wanted to make would require the creation of new software.

  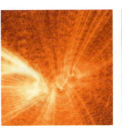 

...oo as musical instrument

usable parameters of
a given particle:

① distance from its
own original source

② magnitude of current
force vector (velocity)

③ absolute left-right
position (stereo...)

④ brightness of pixel
underneath

⑤ deflection from
"original" orient-
ation (what its
orientation would
be if there were
no other sources)

⑥ in-grainedness
– difference in
orientation
between particle's vector
and the gradient of
the image underneath

⑦ absolute orientation & circular pitch

Shepard tones

⑧ distance from cursor.

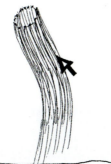

circular

by mapping absolute orientation
to circular pitch:

✳ concentric movement
away from a point
sounds like pure noise
(all frequencies)

✳ "gathered" movement away from
a point sounds like a given
note

✳ rotational movement around
a vortex sounds like transpo-
sition.

(circular)
pitch — orientation of current bearing

volume — magnitude of current bearing:
brightness of substrate ?

timbre — deflection from original bearing ?
(harmonic in-grainedness ?
content)

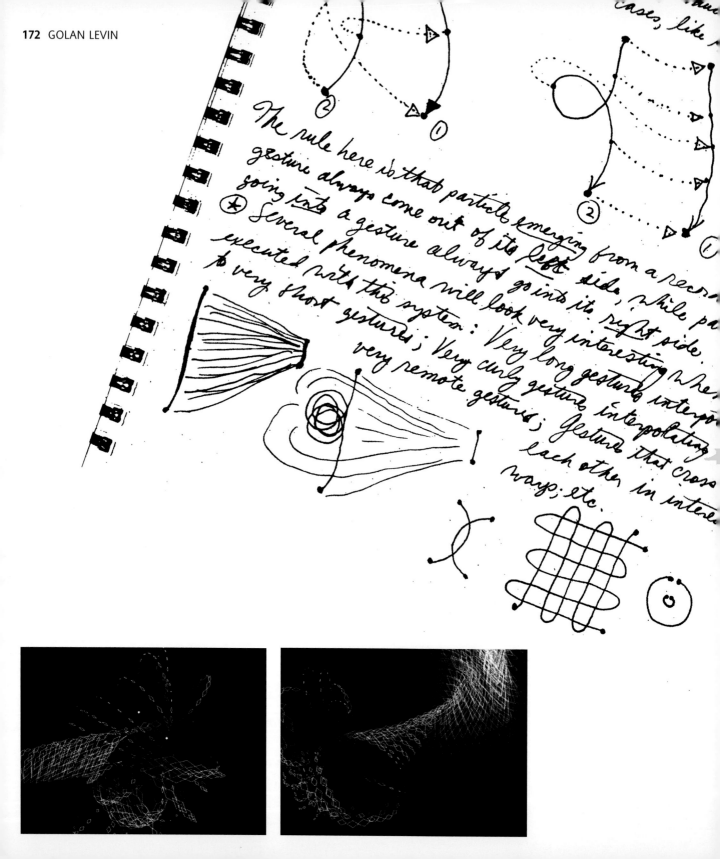

The rule here is that particles emerging from a recta... gesture always come out of its left side, while pa... going into a gesture always go into its right side.

⊛ Several phenomena will look very interesting whe... executed with this system: Very long gestures interpo... to very short gestures; Very curly gestures interpolating very remote gestures; Gestures that cross each other in inter... ways; etc.

DIY design solutions

Not knowing how to write software myself, I first tried a well-worn solution familiar to so many artists new to electronic media – I sought engineering collaborators who could help me implement my visions, so to speak. Engineers are a highly-paid bunch, and this was certainly no less true in Silicon Valley in the mid-1990s. Without money to offer in exchange for their precious engineering time, the most common answer I received was a simple and unequivocal "No."

Occasionally I found an engineer who was between jobs, and who would, astoundingly, agree to help. But I hardly had time to enjoy the collaboration when they would suddenly evaporate: "Sorry man. It's a neat art project but I just got a gig earning $150 an hour." So it happened more than once that I became stranded with half-coded, buggy projects that I could neither fix nor finish myself.

One time I actually found an engineer who was both enthusiastic about my ideas and willing to help me build them. I could hardly believe my luck. I'd give him sketches and then watch over his shoulder while he typed mysterious codes into the computer. "Run it! Run it!" I would say excitedly. He hit a button and we watched the results – and they, umm – *didn't look so good*. No matter how I tried to explain the particular problem, it was nearly impossible to articulate in words that he could understand. The problems were *visual* problems, which I felt and understood in my eye and gut, but could not yet fix or express in the language of the machine.

The final straw was an engineer who let it slip that he was helping me as a kind of charity case: *Oh, you poor, little artist – I'll help you out*. Already frustrated from trying to cajole and bribe engineers into helping me, the feeling of being pitied sent me over the edge. *What am I, stupid?* I refused to believe that programming a computer was some kind of rocket science. I bought the programming books and dug in. That was in 1997.

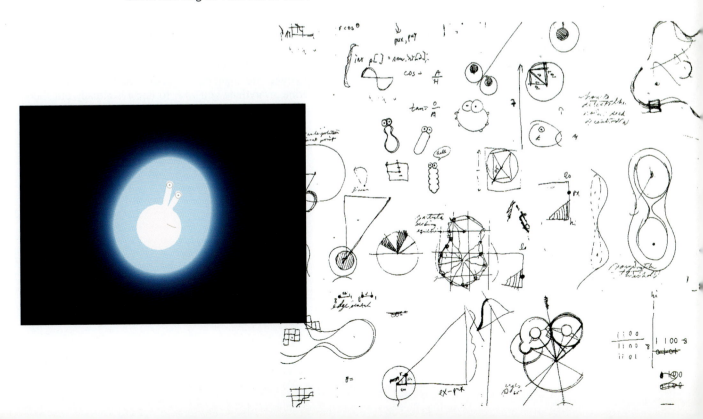

After a year or so of slow progress and false starts, I had learned enough to know that my interests would be artificially constrained if I continued to develop them in a commercial context. In my search for an educational environment that could suit my studies, I seriously considered some art and design schools, but I often found that their approach to the use of technology wasn't rigorous enough. On the other hand, I found many schools in computer science to be boring, impersonal, and focused on tiny ideas.

That was when I heard about a peculiar little course that had just been formed at MIT: Professor John Maeda's Aesthetics and Computation Group at the MIT Media Laboratory. Maeda was unusually committed to encouraging his students to explore their artistic endeavors in a technically rigorous way. He had founded a truly remarkable Studio Art program in Computer Science – a small design school in the heart of a technical university, wherein his students' goals were art and design, but their medium was software. I attended Maeda's program for two years, and continue to recommend it without reservation. (see http://dbn.media.mit.edu for details of his Interactive Java programming environment.)

Nowadays my artwork is developed in the Java and C++ programming languages. I usually do all of my sketches as Java applets for the web, and then develop final pieces in C++ for specially-configured computers. This strategy has worked out pretty well for me – I've been especially satisfied with the way in which the Java sketches, which I post on my web pages online, allow people to get a small taste of what the larger works are like. Of course, there are plenty of other computer languages, each with different toolkits and advantages, and each differently suited to one's personal tastes and goals; the other computational artists I know use an amazing variety of languages, such as Visual Basic, ActionScript, Perl, C, Max and Lingo. But the more computer languages I learn, the more I realize that they're really all the same – much more similar, in fact, than human spoken languages. Regardless of one's preferred computer language choice, I do think it's essential that an artist-of-the-computer-medium should be able to program in some way. For better or worse, it is the only way in which new computer experiences can be made.

Let me end this section of the essay with a brief anecdote. In my last semester of graduate school I was enrolled in two classes. One was entitled The Nature of Mathematical Modeling, taught by MIT physicist Neil Gershenfeld. The curriculum began with second-order partial differential equations, and ended with Hidden Markov Models and cluster-weighted modeling. I hardly understood a word and it nearly fried my brain. It might even have been the most difficult class I had ever taken, were it not for my other course that semester: a course in abstract painting. Now *that* was truly hard. The simple fact is that in visual design, there are no right answers – we have nothing to rely on but our own raw talents and our own eyes. In the realm of software engineering, by contrast, nearly everything one might care to know about or use is available and documented in a book. Programming, computation, engineering: everything you wish to know is already out there, waiting for you to seize it. May you already possess the talents that can't be taught, so that you may learn and use well the ones that can.

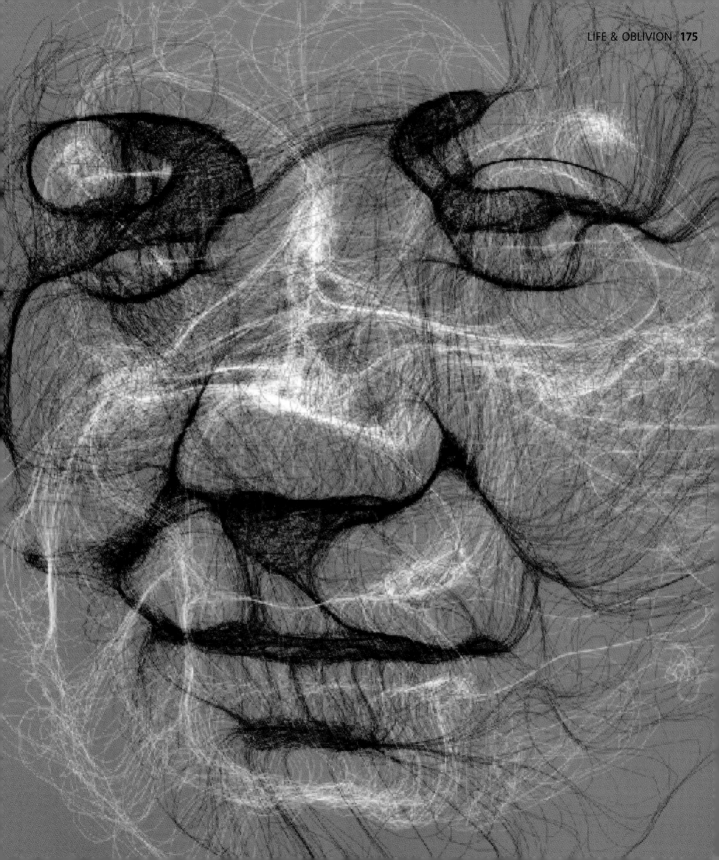

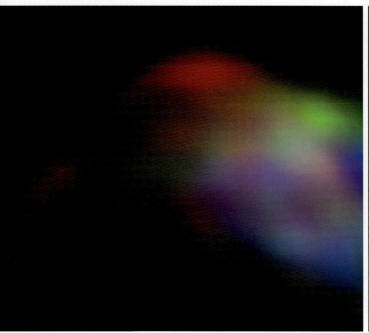
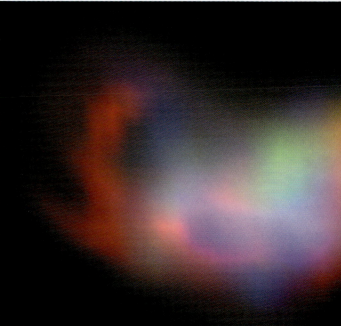

II. Towards Malleable Media

Recently I served on the jury of an interactive media competition, in the course of which we turned our attention to the question: by what metrics shall we evaluate the quality of an interactive artwork? Our interest was more practical than academic – we had several hundred submissions to evaluate and thought it would be helpful to have a short checklist of criteria to keep us focused. Without attempting to be comprehensive, our particular jury reckoned that we cared most about the following issues:

To what extent are the form and content of the work mutually essential in effecting its communication? Are the two wholly inseparable, or is some aspect of either one arbitrary or irrelevant?

How and to what extent are the acts performed by the user, through interaction with the system, socially significant?

What is the depth and character of the feedback loop established between the system and its user?

Entire treatises could be written on any of these questions. The first two of these are chiefly about context, content and communication. Put differently, these two questions ask: when is something worth communicating? And when is it well-communicated? There is no conclusion on these topics that I could possibly present to you here: I entrust the fulfillment of these matters to your own passions, aesthetics and intuitions. The third question, however, is simply one of form. It is the closest to being directly observable, and perhaps the least difficult of the three to discuss and address. And so it is this last criterion – the nature of the human-machine feedback loop – to which I would like to turn our attention.

Interactive systems are deceptive because they wholly and implicitly engulf both static and dynamic media. In this way they masquerade as older forms: if an interactive system moves, it is easy to think it is an animation; if it holds still for a moment, we mistake it for an image. We must not be so easily deceived! Interactive experiences are really quite another thing. They are more than spatial, more than temporal, and more yet, even, than spatiotemporal configurations. The defining property of interactive systems is their use of *feedback* – in which a system's output affects its subsequent input – and their incorporation of *people* as essential components in this feedback cycle.

My thinking on the design of successful interactive feedback systems has been considerably shaped by Marshall McLuhan's famous distinction between what he termed "hot" and "cool" media. To McLuhan, "hot" media are high-definition, high-resolution experiences that are "well-filled with data," while "cool" media are low-definition experiences that leave a great deal of information to be filled in by the mind of the viewer or listener. Within McLuhan's scheme, therefore, photography and film would be examples of hot media, while cartoons and telephony would be cool. McLuhan's definitions establish an opposition between the "temperature" of a medium and the degree to which it invites or requires audience participation: hot media demand little completion by their audience, while cool media, "with their promise of depth involvement and integral expression," are highly participatory.

A quick survey of contemporary visual culture clearly shows a large trend towards the development of high-resolution, high-bandwidth, mega-polygon experiences. The products of this focus – typically photorealistic three-dimensional virtual realities and streaming digital movies – have been dazzling and hypnotizing. But our relations to these spaces are rarely ever more than as spectators, and almost never as creators. The industry's rush to develop these hot experiences, and the expensive machinery they require, has left in its wake numerous fertile and untrammeled technologies for cooler, more participatory media.

My own interest is in the development of sophisticated cool media for interactive communication and personal expression. In pursuing this, I take McLuhan quite literally – that cool media demand completion by a participant. The notable property of cool media, I believe, is that they blur the distinctions between subject and object – between, say, artist and art – enabling the completion of each by the other.

My goal is to understand, build, and encourage systems that blur these boundaries, enabling the flow and communication that is possible when people engage in a transparent, continuous and transformative dialogue with themselves and others. My primary personal criterion for interactive media is, therefore, not the question "for how long can I suspend my disbelief in it?", rather the questions: *for how long can I feel it to be a seamless extension of myself?* – and – *to what depth can I feel connected to another person through it?*

To answer these questions, an interactive medium must become a kind of extension – a sort of prosthesis, which is so adapted to us that our awareness of it drops away when we engage with it. To do this, we must rethink what it means for a medium to be *personal*, for a defining feature of our modern era is that nearly everything we touch or experience is impersonal and canned.

"Canned" is my word for it, anyway. We could just as well describe much of society as pre-prepared or mass-produced. Few aspects of life have been spared from this depressing homogenization. Buildings, food, clothing, furniture, entertainment, even the ground beneath our feet: each unit is rolled off the assembly line or poured out of the vat exactly like every other. But computers have the most unprecedented potential of any technology to respond to us in ways that are uniquely individual.

Computers can see us, listen to us, sense our movements, collect data about us, and read what we write! It is therefore ironic that designers of online art seem to have, for the most part, foregone the opportunities presented by computer input technologies, and instead seized on the computer as yet another mechanism for the delivery and display of pre-prepared content chunks.

To create engaging *interactive* systems that are capable of sustaining our interest over repeated encounters, I believe we must abandon canned materials in favor of creating interesting generative relationships between input and output. When looked at in this way, the number of possible relationships and outcomes is limitless. ...·

No matter what form the user's input takes, there are going to be ways in which it can be amplified, shrunk, sharpened, dulled, embellished, simplified, stored, reversed, echoed, repeated, reflected, slowed, accelerated, rotated, shifted, fragmented, merged, negated, transmitted, transformed, or transmogrified. Taken as a group, these augmentation techniques can be used to present the user with feedback systems whose rules produce surprising and engaging results. If they strike the right balance of intelligibility, novelty and utility, the experience of incorporating oneself into these systems can be deeply enjoyable and perhaps even socially significant.

The creation of generative relationships in interactive artworks is most hampered by the limited malleability of our media. Consider digital audio recordings as an example: there are only a few basic dimensions of a recording that we can easily control, such as its volume and playback speed. With a bit more difficulty, we can modify the recording's overall tone, or even decouple its tempo from its pitch. But unlike a live band, we can't ask the guitarist in a given audio recording to change his melody, or even to stop playing for a moment. In this way, the recording is inflexible and static. To circumvent such limitations in a medium's malleability, a common design strategy is to switch to a related medium which permits control at a finer level of granularity.

In the example of digital sound, we can switch to the use of multi-tracked MIDI instruments – with which we can control the pitch, volume, instrument, and duration of every individual note – or even direct waveform synthesis, with which we can control the most minute details of timbre and sonic texture. The finer our level of granularity, the more control we have, and also the more work we must do to create interesting results. It's a tradeoff that I truly believe is worth making. From the programmer's point of view, we are faced with the choice of triggering something as simple as a "play" button, or doing the hard work of developing a generative synthesis algorithm. But from the user's point of view, we are faced with hearing the *same* melody...*again, and again*...or hearing a sound which responds to our unique presence in the world of information.

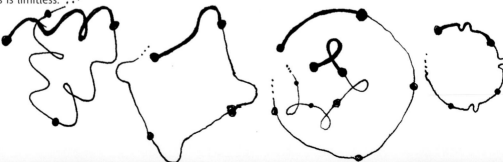

Much of my own work has focused on the development of systems for the real-time creation and performance of animated abstract imagery and synthetic sound. Every environment I develop represents an experimental attempt to design an interface which is at once supple and easy to learn, but which can also yield interesting, infinitely variable and personally expressive performances. In pursuing this goal, I've often found it necessary to use the most malleable media possible, and to build up my generative schemes from first principles. Thus many of my pieces make extended use of low-level synthesis techniques in order to exert direct control over every individual pixel and every sound wave displayed and produced by the computer.

To complete the feedback of the interaction loop, my systems chiefly derive their inputs from human gesture. The psychological and physiological intimacy of the relationship we have with our own gestures is surprising, and when our marks are used to generate uniquely ephemeral dynamic media, it's possible to create simple and transparent interactions which can nevertheless open new vistas of possibility and experience. The pictures which illustrate the following pages are stills taken from my interactive works, and together with the accompanying notes, give an idea of my systems' expressive range.

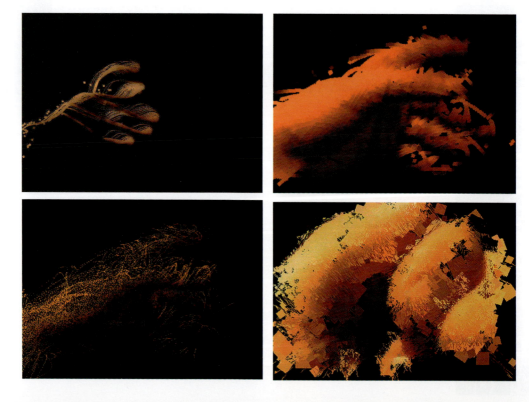

Thoughts on Life and Oblivion

This image is my answer and visual rejoinder to the stated theme of this 4x4 book: *Life & Oblivion*. In this image, I take the stance that life and oblivion are co-requisite points on a single continuum. The sequence was created with a new interactive work called *Dendron*, the subject of my tutorial section.

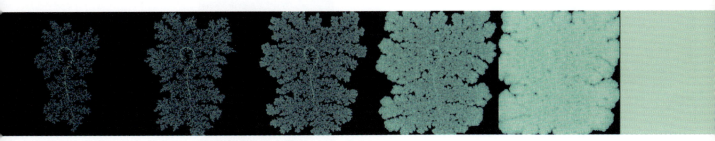

The tutorial is designed to illustrate many of the ideas I've discussed here. It shows the development process behind *Dendron*, a Java applet that allows its user to gesturally manipulate an organic simulation of generative growth. At the technical level, *Dendron*'s implementation presents fractal morphogenesis and pixel-based rendering as a pair of important alternatives to the use of pre-stored imagery. At the aesthetic level, the interactive feedback loop established by *Dendron* straddles order and chaos, life and oblivion.

Directrix (1998). Directrix is an interactive drawing environment in which users can quickly generate animated "pseudo-parabolas." These complex curves are the result of an interplay between a set of dynamic and static gestures performed by the user. When several of these curves are layered together, the results can vary from sparse and delicate constructions of gently curved lines, to violently twitching, thatchy masses.

Directrix creates images from a generalized model of parabolas. In classical geometry, a parabola is defined as the set of points which are equidistant from a special point called the focus, and a straight line called the directrix. The Directrix environment was designed to explore the implications of two premises: firstly, that the shape of a parabola's directrix could be the personal gesture of a user, and secondly, that its focus could be a moving point animated along the trace of a user's recorded gesture. Directrix is interesting because of the interplay it establishes between a strictly spatial specification (the directrix) and a spatio-temporal one (the path of the focus).

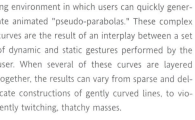

Floo (1999-2001) is an interactive audiovisual environment constructed around a Navier-Stokes simulation of fluid flow. Users create synthetic sounds and images by depositing a series of fluid sources across the terrain of the screen, and then steering a large quantity of particles through the flow field established by these singularities. The image is gradually built up from the luminescent trails left by the particles. The shapes of these trails are entirely a result of the forces originating from the user's cursor and the fluid singularities. As the particles tread again and again over a given location, that spot becomes brighter and brighter.

Escargogolator (1997, collaboration with Scott Snibbe). Escargogolator smoothly exaggerates or diminishes one's strokes, strictly according to their local curvatures. By continually applying transformation to the user's mark – even after its creation is complete – this system allows a user to establish a configuration of gestural "initial conditions," and then observe the manner in which these conditions evolve and devolve over time. Although the strokes inexorably rewind to their points of origin, their movements as they do so are peculiarly wormlike.

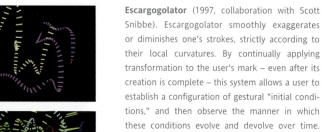

Ribble (1999-2001). Ribble is an interactive application which simulates the flow and dispersal of a gassy medium. When the user drags her cursor around the screen, a trail of gas emerges in its wake, similar to skywriting. A small version is online at: http://acg.media.mit.edu/people/golan/ribble/ .

Meshy (1998) is an interactive drawing environment in which the user's strokes scaffold a gauzy mesh of animated elements. The mesh continally bridges the user's two most recent movements; by making new marks, users can tease and torque the mesh in real-time.

Meshy can be experienced online at:
http://acg.media.mit.edu/people/golan/meshy/

Aurora (1999-2000). It occurred to me that the density map of Floccus' constituent particles might itself make an interesting display. Thus was born Aurora, a reactive system whose structural "underpainting" is a floccular simulation, but whose visual display consists instead of a blurry, shimmering, nebulous cloud. Aurora's glowing formlessness rapidly evolves, dissolves and disperses as it follows and responds to the user's movements.

Floccus (1999) and **Brillo** (1999). In 1999 I began to study the means by which dynamic graphical lines might become able to convey a plausible sense of physicality. After some experimentation I developed a model for representing the underlying structure of "physical" lines, in which a finite-element, mass-spring-damper simulation is composed of virtual particles connected by alternating linear and torsional springs. The model has the effect of simulating the tensile properties of thin physical filaments, such as hairs or twigs.

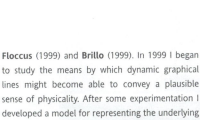

Visionaire Sketches (2001). These are some unpublished sketches for an artwork that eventually appeared in Visionaire 34. The images were created by using gently-randomized sinusoids to control the brightness of each individual pixel.

I used this physical model to create two reactive drawing systems, Brillo and Floccus. In Floccus (the name is a Latin term for "hairball"), ductile filaments drawn by the user swirl around a shifting, imaginary drain centered at the user's cursor. These filaments--torn by conflicting impulses to simultaneously preserve their length, yet also move towards or away from the cursor-- find an equilibrium by forming gnarly, tangled masses.

In Brillo, filaments drawn by the user are buffeted by forces derived from a hidden but underlying photograph. Light-colored filaments are attracted to bright regions of the photograph, while dark filaments are attracted to dark regions. I used these simple rules to coalesce piles of casual scribbles into several portraits of my colleagues. The results are wispy, organic and sometimes unsettling transformations: chiaroscuros in hair.

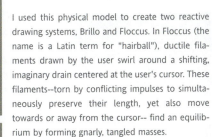

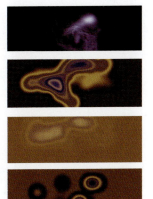

Dakadaka (1999, collaboration with Casey Reas). Typing can be thought of as a percussive spatial action – a play of tiny thoughts scattered onto a tightly organized grid. On the other hand, typing is also a kind of speech, spoken through the fingers with flashing rhythms and continuous gestures. Dakadaka is an interactive Java applet that explores these two ideas by combining positional typographic systems with an abstract dynamic display. One can understand Dakadaka as a prototype for an ambient display which could augment one's ordinary typing as an auxiliary, transparent layer in an attempt to infuse typography with the fleeting dynamics of speech. Alternatively, one can also understand Dakadaka as an experience in its own right, re-framing the act of typing at a computer keyboard as a visual exploration.

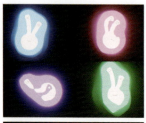

Obzok (2001) is a creature created for the January 2001 issue of singlecell.org, a monthly online bestiary. Singlecell features a variety of virtual creatures discovered and reared by a diverse group of computational artists and designers. See http://www.singlecell.org/ .

Flingerflow (1998). Flingerflow, one of my exercises from Maeda's class in computational photography, was a study in bringing a photograph of a hand to life. I placed a few hundred particles on the surface of each hand photograph, and let the particles guide themselves across the gradients of the hand's surface. The images are built up from the trails of the travelling particles.

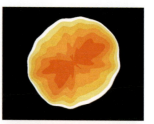

Slamps (2000) are a series of dynamic app intended to be projected as "lamps", w react to the loudness and frequency conten ambient sound. Slamps can be downloaded Windows PCs from http://acg.media.mit.edu/ ple/golan/slamps/

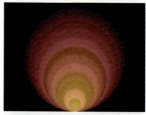

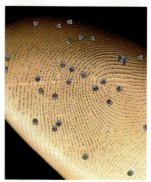

Fingerbahn (1998). The Fingerbahn is a visua tion of all the little buggies who spend their on our hides.The user can give each of the bug a unique starting position; immediately th begin to move along the grooves of my fin prints. To make the Fingerbahn I computed a field from each fingerprint; the buggies then c mute back and forth along this flow field.

Cubescape (1999). One day Maeda, bored of all my 2D works, forced me to create something in 3D. It didn't feel natural. This was the failed experiment that resulted.

Splat (1998). A group of friendly blobs obligingly merge under the user's control. Inplicit curves provide a pleasantly gooey edge. To experience the piece, please visit:

http://acg.media.mit.edu/people/golan/splat/

Puttypix (1998). Puttypix was an interactive system I developed for Maeda's photography course. We had to use code to "bring our favorite thing to life" – in my case, Silly Putty. I developed a basic shape grammar that allowed small putty photographs to interconnect, guaranteeing that their overall edge would always be continuous and smooth. See http://acg.media.mit.edu/people/golan/photo/ps6/

Molassograph (1998). The Molassograph gradually reveals an image-gestalt through the contractions and rarefactions of the user's moving particles. Where the underlying image is darker, the particles move more slowly, making little traffic jams; where the underlying image is lighter, the particles move more quickly. See http://acg.media.mit.edu/people/golan/photo/ps5/

Curly (1998-2000) repeats a user's strokes end-over-end, enabling simultaneous specification of a line's shape and quality of movement. Each line repeats according to its own period, producing an ever-changing yet consistent animated texture. The result is an animated and responsive display of lively, worm-like lines.

Curly is available as a downloadable executable for Windows PCs: http://acg.media.mit.edu/people/golan/curly/ .

Streamer (1997, developed in collaboration with Scott Snibbe) began as an attempt to design a "kite" guided by the cursor. I chose to represent the long string of a kite as a graphical line emitted by the cursor, as in a traditional drawing program, but which is also progressively smoothed at every frame of animation, according to a naive simulation of kitestring physics. In the course of developing this simulation, I accidentally introduced a sign error, and the progressive smoothing I had intended became an exponential amplification instead! The positive feedback of this process results in a rapid exaggeration of the user's gesture, with the mark's trail overlapping itself and quickly flying away in all directions. Even the tiniest wiggles in the user's gesture are magnified to the entire breadth of the screen within a few fractions of a second. The effect is an intoxicatingly responsive chaos, similar to the experience of driving too fast.

The most important contribution of **Polygona Nervosa** (1997) is the idea that a single interaction can be used to specify both the spatial and temporal aspects of a animated visual form. The system achieves this by leveraging the different affordances of the discrete and continuous aspects of a mouse-gesture: discrete mouse clicks are used to specify the shapes' spatial forms and positions, while continuous mouse movements are used to specify spatio-temporal dynamics.

Stripe (1998) allows its user to paint "chemicals" into a reaction-diffusion simulation. Such simulations are believed to model the formation of leopard spots and zebra stripes; here, their result is a kaliedoscopic pattern of subtly-evolving gradients.

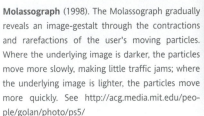

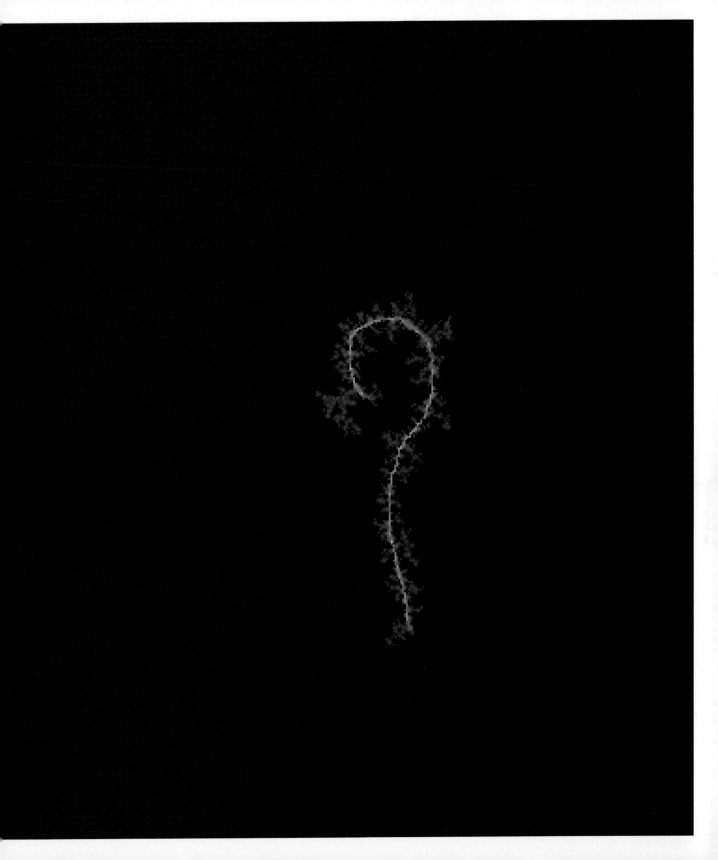

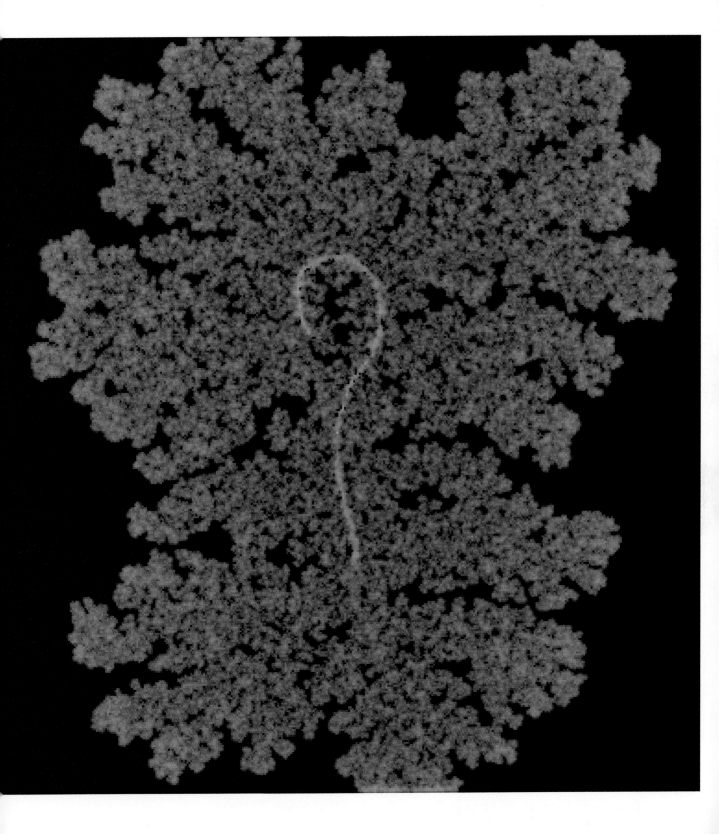

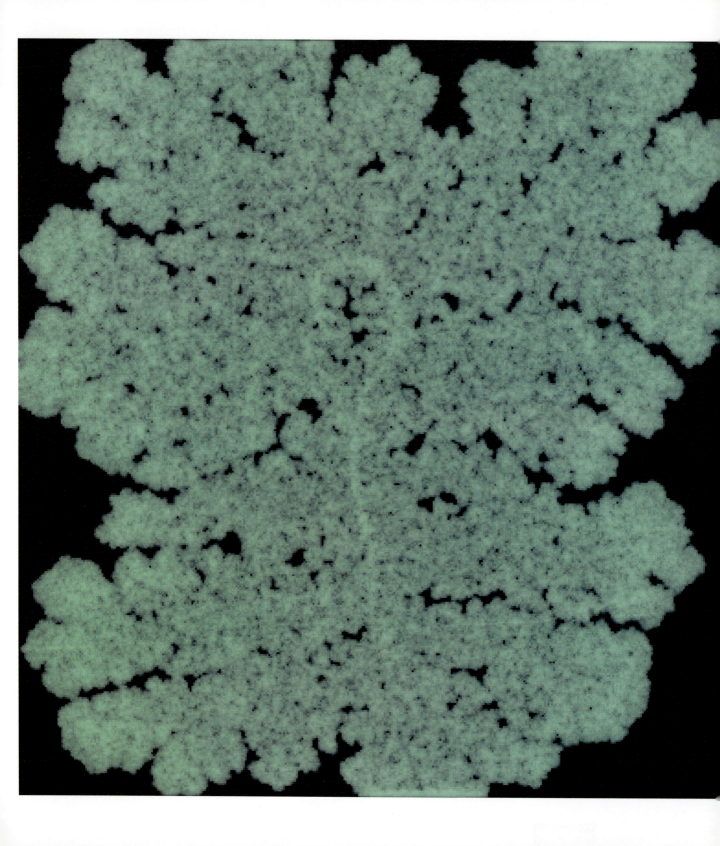

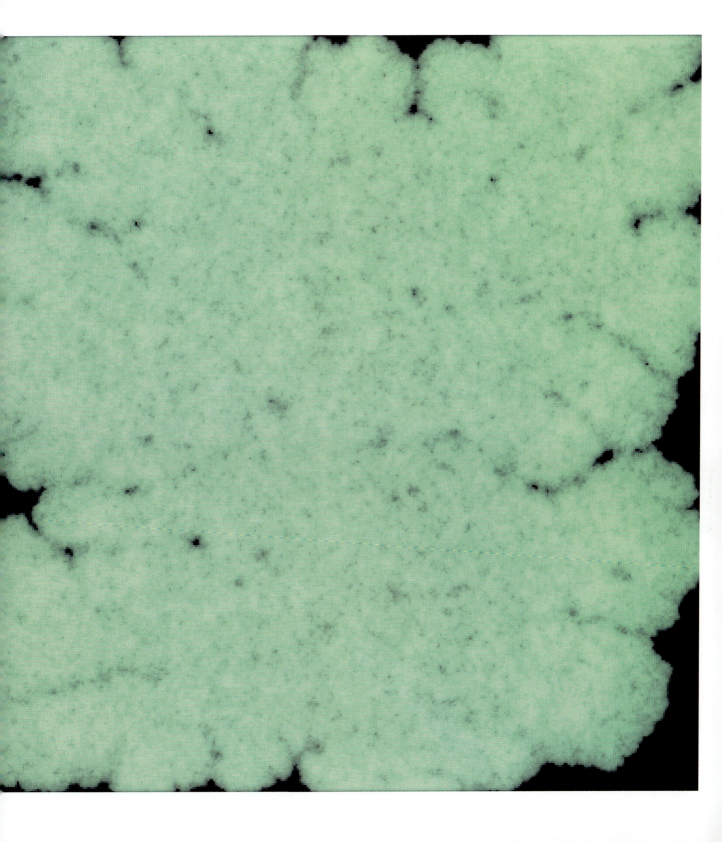

Dendron: Painting with Fungus

In this tutorial, I'll present the development process behind Dendron, a new interactive system. It allows its user to engage with a reactive animated simulation of organic growth – indeed, it takes its name from the dendritic (or treelike) growth that occurs in its framework. In Dendron, the user draws with the cursor to produce a series of linear marks on the system's canvas. Over time, these marks are used to scaffold the growth of a delicately filigreed structure of fingerlike branches.

The generative algorithm on which Dendron is based – called Diffusion-Limited Aggregation, or DLA – is surprisingly simple, and probably more difficult to pronounce than to understand. Variations of DLA are often used to model the growth of lichen, molds, root systems, and certain kinds of crystalline minerals. So you may find the experience of using Dendron a bit like painting with fungus.

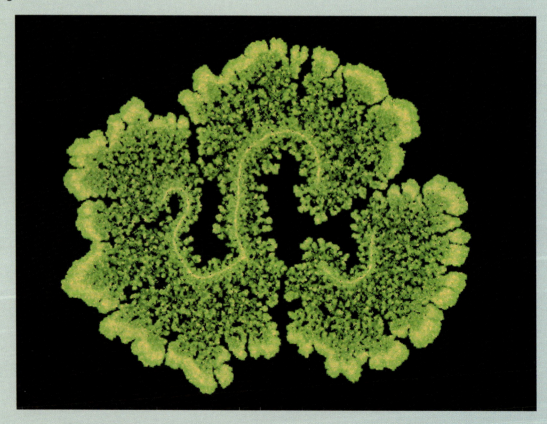

The first reaction you may have is: Gross! Why a tutorial in painting with fungus?

In fact, there are three reasons why I've chosen to present this particular piece.

Dendron is an interactive artwork – it is also a kind of paint program, one that you can make yourself. Although its repertoire of tools may be limited, Dendron's means are also unique: by comparison, for better or for worse, Photoshop has no Fungus Tool. By presenting the software development process of a paint program like Dendron, I hope to encourage you to make your own paint programs, each with its own special characteristics.

Another reason for looking at Dendron is that its pixel-based means are a direct contrast to the overwhelming tide of interactive works. Because the most popular authoring environments have been optimized to deal with stored images (Director) and vector artwork (Flash), there aren't many examples, especially online, of interactive artworks that deal directly with individual pixels.

The third reason I've chosen to discuss Dendron stems from my belief that coded manipulation of low-level media can enable the creation of some unique interactive experiences. The use of "canned" component materials, such as pre-prepared sounds and videos, often leads to disappointingly repetitive interactive experiences. In Dendron, there are no pre-prepared assets (the entire applet fits into a 5k download!). Instead, Dendron places the user into a dialog with an algorithm. The possible outcomes are innumerable, intimately tied to the user's input, and always different.

Dendron was initially written in the form of a Java applet: some time later, I ported it to the C++ language and used the OpenGL graphics library instead of Java's default graphics library. This tutorial presents the Java version, but I'd like to point out that Dendron could actually have been written in any coding environment with a graphics toolkit that allows for the reading and writing of individual pixel values. I'll give an example of this later.

For the most part, this tutorial assumes that you have a rudimentary familiarity with basic programming techniques. If you've never even seen Java before, don't fret – most programming languages are astonishingly similar. If you're interested in getting your hands dirty with the Dendron code itself, you'll have to know a bit about how to compile a Java file. Although this information is beyond the scope of this tutorial, it is widely available from many other sources. For Mac users who are new to Java, let me add that you'll always get the best results if you download the latest Macintosh Runtime for Java (MRJ plugin) from http://www.apple.com/java. PC users can download a Java platform from http://java.sun.com/. If you're not a programmer, I hope this tutorial gives you an insight into what kinds of processes go into producing the programs you use, and inspires you to try out some for yourself.

A Simulation of Dendritic Growth

Dendron's core principle is called DLA, or Diffusion-Limited Aggregation. DLA is now considered to be one of the most important models of fractal morphogenesis. As such, it has been used to model an enormous variety of natural phenomena characterized by dendritic growth, such as the development of frost on a windowpane, crystals, urban sprawl, lichen and fungi, coral, and lightning. Its growth rule is remarkably simple, as you can see from the diagram.

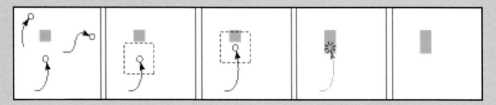

In this illustration of the DLA algorithm, you can see we start with an immobile seed pixel (the gray square) in the image plane, surrounded by a number of wandering particles (circles). If a particle comes close enough to the seed, it is immobilized instantly and deposits a new pixel.

In DLA, particles of a given resource diffuse freely in a region until they are captured by – and contribute to the growth of – a static structure. Suppose there is a territory populated with particles of nutrients, randomly circulating. These nutrients are required by a simple growing structure (such as a bacterial colony) to form its body. When a particle collides with the colony structure, it gets stuck to it, adding to its perimeter. As this process continues, more and more particles collide with the structure, and its shape evolves accordingly. That's all there is to it, though differences in the way the particles move around will govern whether the resulting structure is shaped more like a tree (with delicate branches) or a Jawbreaker candy (with many spherical layers).

The DLA algorithm is well-described by the following bit of pseudocode, in which the aggregated structure in question is not a bacterial colony, but an assembly of darkened pixels on the screen:

```
for every particle P
    if P is in the vicinity of a darkened pixel
        deposit another darkened pixel in P's location
        and delete P
    otherwise
        have P continue to move around randomly
    end if
end for
```

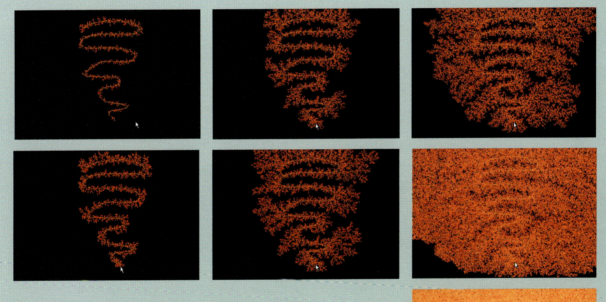

In the Dendron applet, the initial structure is a mark drawn each time the user drags the cursor across the canvas and a thin line of pixels is darkened (or lightened) in an otherwise blank image. Soon, more pixels are deposited around the edges of the user's marks – the result of tens of thousands of invisible particles wandering across the screen. The initial scribbles develop buds, then branches, and then trunklike offshoots. They may even grow to fill the screen completely.

Getting and Setting Pixels

Although Diffusion-Limited Aggregation is a fairly simple generative algorithm, the pseudocode above does gloss over some important technical details. How can one know, for example, whether or not particle P is in the vicinity of a darkened pixel? If it is, how does one deposit another darkened pixel in P's location? These two questions touch on the most fundamental requirements of any pixel-oriented graphics programming environment: we must have the ability to query (get) and assign (set) the contents of individual pixels. This means we need to understand what a pixel is, and how the numeric information contained in it is actually stored and represented by a computer.

So what are pixels? Well, the word pixel was coined in the 1960s from a contraction of the words "picture element". They are small units that make up larger pictures. But pixels are much more than mere daubs of paint or grains of film. They are conceptual units for representing digital information. Like all data structures in the computer, they are invisible and therefore require an output device to be seen.

MIT researcher Kelly Heaton has pointed out that pixels, most often made physical as glowing phosphor elements in a CRT screen, "can just as well be visualized through light bulbs or actuated tiles or swarming ants or any other discrete unit that can be made to change visibly in response to digital information." Heaton mentions Eric Staller's Lightmobile (a VW bug studded with 1700 flickering lightbulbs) and Danny Rozin's magnificent Wooden Mirror (a mechanical sculpture which controls the movements of 840 wooden tiles from real-time video input) as novel examples of physical pixel implementations. Although I assume that your display is a traditional computer monitor, it is important to understand that a pixel is really nothing more than a piece of data.

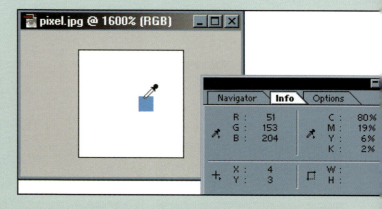

Have you ever seen, probed or manipulated a single pixel? If you're a Photoshop user, you're probably a seasoned expert at this, and you'll be familiar with the interface above. In this screenshot, I've used Photoshop's Eyedropper tool to sample the color of a single (highly magnified) bluish pixel. At the same time I've opened Photoshop's Info Display window to reveal the numeric data associated with that pixel. This tells me that this particular pixel is located 4 horizontal units from the left edge of the image, and 3 vertical units from the top of the image. I can also tell that, in order to display this particular pixel correctly, the intensity of the monitor's Red beam is set to an intensity of 51 (out of a possible 255), while the Green and Blue beams are set to intensities of 153 and 204, respectively. Clearly, each little pixel represents a group of numbers resident somewhere in the computer's memory.

It's rare that we need to worry about these individual numbers when we use Photoshop or other paint programs. There are just too many pixels to count! If we had to think about all of the numbers involved whenever we wanted to create a Drop Shadow or remove some red-eye from a snapshot, we'd soon go crazy. But when we want to create our own paint program, we must confront the stark fact that these numbers are all we have to work with. To create our own pixel-processing software we need to dig down to this lower level of pure numbers, and get to know the way in which pixels are stored, accessed, manipulated and represented.

John Maeda's Design By Numbers (DBN) programming environment, available at http://dbn.media.mit.edu/, provides one of the simplest mechanisms for getting and setting the values of pixels, and is therefore a sensible starting point. The DBN graphics universe is entirely played out on a grid of 100 x 100 pixels in a strictly grayscale palette, the values of which range from 0 (white) to 100 (black). In Maeda's language, the brightness of a pixel located at [x y] is set to a grayscale value g, using the syntax:

```
set [x y] g
```

DBN's method for retrieving the value of a pixel is just as simple: here, the variable g is assigned to have the grayscale value already stored in the pixel located at [x y]:

```
set g [x y]
```

Here a cluster of four pixels in the center of the DBN canvas is set to black:

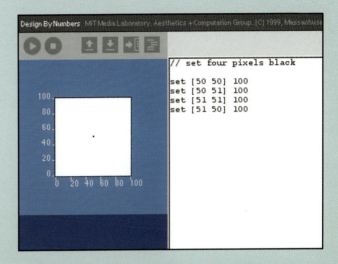

Design By Numbers is frequently used as an introductory
programming language in design schools because of its
immediate, results-oriented approach to computation.
Although it is extremely simple, it is also a full-featured
language, with all of the amenities we need to create a
DLA-simulation program like Dendron. To show Dendron
implemented in another language besides Java, here is a
DBN version of Dendron's code:

```
// Dendron.dbn by Golan Levin, October 2001.
// A program for simulating Diffusion-Limited Aggregation.
// To execute this program, visit:
// http://dbn.media.mit.edu/

// In DBN, we have to create our own function
// for generating random numbers... sigh.
// This is a Linear Feedback Shift Register
// technique for generating random numbers.
set bb 198621
set mm 98621
set seed 73
number random
{
    set bl (seed*bb+1)
    set seed (bl % mm)
    value (seed % 100)
}

// Use the DBN array to store the coordinates of N=100 Particles.
// Array indices 1 to N will store the X-coordinates, while
// array indices (N+1) to (N+N) will store the Y-coordinates.
set N 100
repeat a 1 N
{
    set b (a+N)
    set <array a> ((<random>/2)+50)
    set <array b> ((<random>/2)+50)
}

// Here we initialize some graphics properties
set mx <mouse 1>
set my <mouse 2>
norefresh
pen 100
paper 0

// Here's the main loop, which runs forever.
forever
{
    set prevx mx
    set prevy my
    set mx <mouse 1>
```

```
set my <mouse 2>
set mb <mouse 3>
same? mb 100
{
    line prevx prevy mx my
}
// refresh the screen
refresh

// process the DLA algorithm if the user is not busy drawing
notsame? mb 100
{

    // for every particle stored in the array
    repeat a 1 N
    {
        // get the coordinates of the particle
        set b (a+N)
        set x2 <array a>
        set y2 <array b>

        // and derive the coordinates of
        // the particle's neighboring pixels
        set x1 (x2 - 1)
        set y1 (y2 - 1)
        set x3 (x2 + 1)
        set y3 (y2 + 1)

        // compute the sum of the contents of
        // the particle's neighboring pixels
        set sum        ([x1 y1] + [x2 y1] + [x3 y1])
        set sum (sum + [x1 y2] + [x2 y2] + [x3 y2])
        set sum (sum + [x1 y3] + [x2 y3] + [x3 y3])

        // if the sum is greater than some threshold,
        // then darken the pixel under the particle,
        // thus adding to the aggregate structure.
        notsmaller? sum 10
        {
            set [x2 y2] 90
        }

        // move the particles in a random direction
        set dx (<random> / 20)
        set dy (<random> / 20)

        // update the positions of the particles
        set <array a> ((x2 + dx)%100)
        set <array b> ((y2 + dy)%100)
    }
}
}
```

It's a vaguely perverse programming tool to use, since the DBN interpreter is so slow, and its imaging region is so small. But its results are happily consistent with those from our Java version:

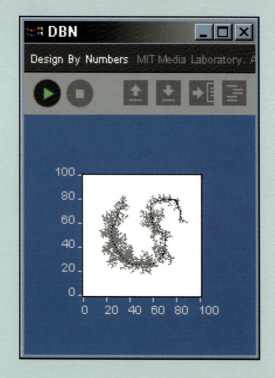

DBN, Java and OpenGL aren't the only programming environments that allow designers to get and set the value of individual pixels. Macromedia's Director environment includes new Lingo commands for this important functionality. Setting a pixel in Lingo requires two lines of code:

```
— Fetch an image out of a cast member
anImage = member("someCastName").image

— Set the pixel at location (x,y) in the image to (red,green,blue)
image.setPixel(point(x,y),rgb(red, green, blue))
```

Likewise, Lingo makes it possible to obtain the RGB color stored in a given pixel as well:

```
— Fetch the image out of a cast member
anImage = sprite(me.spriteNum).member.image

— Get an rgb data structure from a pixel's contents
aColor = anImage.getPixel(col,row)
```

Pixel manipulation in Director hasn't seen wide acceptance yet, but a few designers have already made some important online works with it. Charles Forman, who runs the design site www.setpixel.com, has created some highly sophisticated pixel-based Director pieces, and he provides source files for many interesting raster-based experiments. For the time being, however, serious pixel manipulations in Director are relatively slow, and are not likely to find broad appeal with designers until their speed is practical for full-frame animation.

©Charles Forman www.setpixel.com (subpixel demo)

My own casual comparisons of pixel operations in the different programming environments, performed on my reasonably humble 733 Mhz Pentium, showed that I could perform about 2000 individual pixel operations per second in DBN, 300,000 per second in Director, 4 million per second in Java, and 15 million per second in C++ with OpenGL. Programmers willing to write code in x86 Assembler can get even higher rates. Naturally, Dendron's DLA algorithm will work in any of these environments. But in the interest of both space and time, I'll leave the Director and Assembler versions as an exercise for the reader, and jump in – finally – to Java.

In Java there is no pre-defined method to extract or set the value of a pixel. Instead, we have to create our own functions for doing so. The inner workings of these functions will depend on how we configure the memory that stores the pixels: will we use a two-dimensional array or a one-dimensional array? Will we use bytes in combination with an 8-bit indexed color palette, or integers in combination with a 24-bit full-color palette? In the code snippet below, I set up the pixel array, and present a version of these functions where I have chosen to represent our pixels with a one-dimensional array of bytes. This configuration, incidentally, is the speediest of all of our options.

```java
int       rasterWidth = 640;      // Declare the integer width of the pixel field.

int       rasterHeight = 480;     // Declare the integer height of the pixel field.

byte      rasterPixels[];         // Declare an array of bytes that stores pixel values.

void allocateSomePixelMemory(){
                            // Allocate the memory needed by the array of pixel values.
      rasterPixels = new byte[rasterWidth * rasterHeight];
}

int getPixel (int x, int y){
   // Extract a byte from a certain location in the pixel array.
// Note that we have to compute the pixel's index in the 1-
// dimensional array, as a function of x and y. We also have to
//convert the signed byte to an unsigned integer with the 0xFF
// bitwise operation.

   int loc = y*rasterWidth + x;
   return (0xFF & rasterPixels[loc]);
}

void setPixel (int x, int y, byte b){
   int loc = y*rasterWidth + x;
   rasterPixels[loc] = b;
}
```

Dendron in Java

In this tutorial, I intersperse the code to the Dendron applet with my own discussions about its mechanism and construction. The code is also reproduced in an uninterrupted form, available for download at http://www.friendsofed.com/4x4/generative/source/.

Dendron's Java code is about a thousand lines long. You may well ask, how did it get to be so large, when the equivalent program in DBN is less than a hundred lines? In fact, the relevant chunks of code which perform the DLA simulation are almost exactly the same size in both languages! The difference is due to the fact that, in Java, we are obliged to set up and create more of our own resources.

Preparation

While DBN automatically gives us a Pixel Field and a Color Palette, working in Java requires us to create everything from scratch. More than 80% of our Java code is therefore devoted to the common sorts of setup tasks that must be made, time and time again, with every applet. The tradeoff for all of this extra work, naturally, is that Java offers us greater flexibility and speed.

At the very beginning of the program code, we import a standard set of Java libraries. These libraries will give us the functionality we need to create an applet, and also to allow us to use Java's graphics features. Of particular importance is the first line, which provides us with the ability to use Java's advanced imaging features, such as pixel-based imaging and custom palette creation. These libraries are built in to the Java language and development environment.

```
import java.awt.image.*;
import java.applet.*;
import java.awt.*;
```

Now the Dendron call itself is declared. This Java class extends Applet, meaning that it inherits all of the properties and affordances of a generic applet. Our constructor also stipulates that the Dendron class is Runnable, which allows it to perform (threaded) interactive animation.

```
public class Dendron extends Applet
implements Runnable {
```

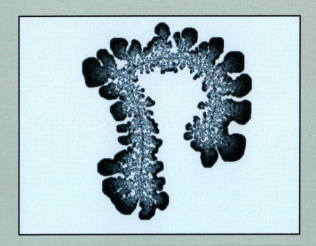

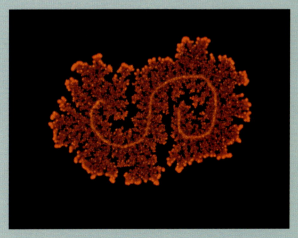

We now begin the process of declaring the applet's global variables, in order to allocate the computer memory we will need to store its information. Note that declaring a variable or object is not the same as initializing it (this will be covered later); Java encourages us to do these tasks separately.

I've grouped the applet's variables into three sections, loosely according to whether the variables are just used to set up the basic plumbing of the applet, or whether they are used in the applet's pixel-based imaging, or whether they store data about the Diffusion-Limited Aggregation simulation. If you're not familiar with Java, it may be helpful to know that Java is a strongly-typed language, meaning that every declared variable must be introduced by a special keyword that indicates the kind of data the variable stores.

Our first group of declarations stores some of the applet's general plumbing, such as its colors, current and previous mouse positions, animation Thread, and so on. In the lines below, we therefore declare that we will need two Color objects, four integers, a Thread object, a boolean (true or false) value, and another integer. It should become clear that Java uses the pair of slashes (//) as an escape sequence to indicate a comment in the code.

```
Color   myBackgroundColor;          // The raster's background Color.
Color   myForegroundColor;          // The raster's foreground Color.
int     mouseX;                 // the mouse's horizontal coordinate.
int     mouseY;                 // The mouse's vertical coordinate.
int     prevMouseX;                 // The mouse's previous X-location.
int     prevMouseY;                 // The mouse's previous Y-location.

Thread animationThread = null;      // The Thread which powers the animation.

boolean stopAnimationThread;        // A flag which stops the animation thread
    int     threadSleepTime = 25;       // The number of milliseconds between frames.
```

In the next lines, we declare the global objects and variables that will be used in our applet's raster-based imaging method. In addition to the integers, note that we also declare an array of bytes (which will eventually contain the pixel data), a couple of `Image` objects, and an `IndexColorModel` object which will serve as our palette of colors. Finally, we declare that we will need a `MemoryImageSource` object – a special object that plays an important role in connecting all of these elements together. The definitions for objects like the `IndexColorModel` and the `MemoryImageSource`, incidentally, were made available to us when we imported the Java image libraries at the head of the code; you can find more information about them in any good Java book.

```
int     rasterWidth;              // The width of the applet's pixel field.
int     rasterHeight;             // The height of the applet's pixel field.
byte    rasterPixels[];           // The array of bytes containing the pixels.
                                  // Note that arrays are declared with brackets [].
int     numberOfRasterPixels;     // The size (length) of this byte array.

Image   rasterImage;              // A Java Image object made from rasterPixels.
Image   appletImage;              // The Applet's main image, into which we
                                  // will periodically paint the rasterImage

IndexColorModel myPalette;        // An indexed-color palette we will construct.

MemoryImageSource myMIS;          // A special Java object which creates the
                                  // connection between the (rasterPixels) byte
                                  // array, the (myPalette) IndexColorModel,
                                  // and the (rasterImage) output Image.
```

Now we declare the variables and objects we will use in Dendron's Diffusion-Limited Aggregation (DLA) simulation.

You will recall that DLA fractals emerge from of a set of particles that travel around the main raster of pixels: here we set some of the properties of those particles, including an important set of constants. Modifications to these numbers will yield substantial differences in the behavior of the applet. They are powerful tools for customizing the applet, and understanding its mechanism.

```
int             numberOfParticles;
Particle        particleArray[];

float aggregationThreshold = 32;      // The threshold necessary for a Particle to get
                                      //stuck to the aggregate structure.

float maxParticleVelocity = 20;       // The Particles' top speed.

byte DRAW_BYTE = (byte)92;            // The byte representing the palette index of the
                                      //color we will draw with.

byte ACCRETE_BYTE = (byte)48;             // The byte representing the palette index
                                          //of the color that pixels will accrete with.

int blurFrequency = 5;                    // How often we'll blur a fragment of the
                                          //simulation's structure. Higher numbers
                                          //yield less frequent blurring.

final int UNSIGN = 0xFF;               // A special constant which will help us properly
                                       //fetch byte values out of the pixel array.
```

We have finished declaring our variables and objects, and so it is now time to compose functions which instantiate and manipulate them.

A sensible place to start is the `init` method, which is the applet's main initialization call. `init` is automatically executed whenever the applet is launched in a web browser – you'll never need to call the method yourself. As it is written here, `init` first sets up the applet's graphics resources, and then initializes the DLA simulation:

```
public void init(){
        initializeImaging();
        initializeSimulation();
}
```

Next is the `initializeImaging` method, called by `init` in the first moments of the applet's existence. This method performs a great deal of important initializations!

It begins by reading in some size and color parameters from the HTML page in which the applet is embedded. After this, the function creates our customized color palette, creates our pixel raster's byte array, and creates a variety of other appropriately-sized resources. One especially important initialization is that of the `MemoryImageSource`, called `myMIS`, that we declared earlier: this special object is the glue which will bind together our `rasterPixels` array of pixel data to the `IndexColorModel` palette that will color it.

```
void initializeImaging(){
        // First, read in the applet's parameter tags from the HTML page.
        // These will be used to set the applet's dimensions and colors,
        // which are stored in a variety of global variables, including
        // rasterWidth, rasterHeight, myBackgroundColor and myForegroundColor.
        readAppletParameters();

        // Resize the applet to be the same size as our raster area.
        this.resize (rasterWidth, rasterHeight);

        // Create the applet's main Image.
        appletImage = createImage (rasterWidth, rasterHeight);

        // Create the IndexColorModel, myPalette, which will be
        // used as the palette for all of our imaging.
        createCustomPalette();

        // Create the array of bytes which will
        // store the image we are computing.
        numberOfRasterPixels = rasterWidth * rasterHeight;
        rasterPixels = new byte[numberOfRasterPixels];

        // Initialize the rasterPixels[] array,
        // so that all pixels are zero to begin with.
        for (int i=0; i<numberOfRasterPixels; i++){
                rasterPixels[i] = (byte) 0;
        }

        // Create myMIS, a MemoryImageSource. This is a special Java object
        // which establishes a relationship between a given array of bytes
        // and a given IndexColorModel, such that taken together they can be
        // interpreted as a source of displayable images.
```

```
        myMIS = new MemoryImageSource(rasterWidth,
                                      rasterHeight,
                                      myPalette,
                                      rasterPixels,
                                      0, rasterWidth);

        // This line of code establishes that myMIS can be used for
        // creating animated pixel displays, which is the case here.
        myMIS.setAnimated(true);

        // This line of code updates myMIS with the latest values from
        // the array of bytes, rasterPixels.
        myMIS.newPixels(0, 0, rasterWidth, rasterHeight);

        // Finally, we create the Java Image object which will actually
        // display our pixels. rasterImage is an Image whose pixels are
        // stored as bytes in the rasterPixels array, and whose pixels are
        // interpreted by the color palette stored in myPalette.
        rasterImage = createImage(myMIS);

    }
```

The readAppletParameters method is a special subroutine, called by initializeImaging above, which fetches important information from the parameter tags in the applet's accompanying HTML page.

In Java, parameter values are read as Strings, so it's necessary to convert them into the data types we want (such as integers and Color objects) before we can use them. This method calls another subroutine, stringToColor, to handle the matter of converting the web's hexadecimal color strings into Java's native Color objects.

```
    void readAppletParameters() {
        String widthValue      = getParameter("width");
        String heightValue     = getParameter("height");
        String backgroundValue = getParameter("background");
        String foregroundValue = getParameter("foreground");

        // Put in a sanity check, just in case the applet tags
        // were accidentally left blank, or are not parsable.
        if (widthValue == null)       { widthValue      = "320"; }
        if (heightValue == null)      { heightValue     = "240"; }
        if (backgroundValue == null)  { backgroundValue = "000000"; }
        if (foregroundValue == null)  { foregroundValue = "FFFFFF"; }
```

```
            rasterWidth  = Integer.parseInt(widthValue);
            rasterHeight = Integer.parseInt(heightValue);
            myBackgroundColor = stringToColor(backgroundValue);
            myForegroundColor = stringToColor(foregroundValue);
    }


    Color stringToColor(String hexString) {
            // This helper function converts a String formatted
            // as "RRGGBB" into a Java Color object, which it returns.
            int red   = (Integer.decode("0x" + hexString.substring(0,2))).intValue();
            int green = (Integer.decode("0x" + hexString.substring(2,4))).intValue();
            int blue  = (Integer.decode("0x" + hexString.substring(4,6))).intValue();

            Color convertedColor = new Color (red, green, blue);
            return convertedColor;
    }
```

The `createCustomPalette` method is a simple yet useful function, which is also called from within the `initializeImaging` procedure. It creates an indexed palette of 256 colors by interpolating between the foreground and background colors loaded from the HTML parameters.

In order to enhance the character of the intermediate colors, three emphasis factors are used to non-linearly distort the interpolation. The result is a palette (an `IndexColorModel` object) that blends from one color to another in a subtle and interesting way.

```
    void createCustomPalette(){
            // Create the palette we'll use to display the pixels.
            // This 256-color palette blends between the background and foreground
            // colors that were specified in the HTML parameter tags. We assume that
            // readAppletParameters() has already been called, which reads these
            // parameters into the myBackgroundColor and myForegroundColor objects.

            // Fetch the individual color components of myBackgroundColor
            float r0 = (float) myBackgroundColor.getRed();
            float g0 = (float) myBackgroundColor.getGreen();
            float b0 = (float) myBackgroundColor.getBlue();

            // Fetch the individual color components of myForegroundColor
            float r1 = (float) myForegroundColor.getRed();
            float g1 = (float) myForegroundColor.getGreen();
            float b1 = (float) myForegroundColor.getBlue();
```

```
// Allocate arrays for 256 red, green and blue values.
byte rArray[] = new byte[256];
byte gArray[] = new byte[256];
byte bArray[] = new byte[256];

// Fill the red, green and blue arrays with values that
// blend from myBackgroundColor to myForegroundColor.

// Use non-linear color scaling factors to create a more interesting
// palette. Values of 1 will provide linear interpolation; values less
// than 1 will emphasize, and values greater than 1 will de-emphasize.
// Note the 'f', which indicates that these are floats and not doubles.
float rEmphasis = 0.1f;
float gEmphasis = 0.6f;
float bEmphasis = 0.9f;

for (int i=0; i<256; i++) {
        float percent  = (float) (i/255.0);
        float rPercent = (float) Math.pow(percent, rEmphasis);
        float gPercent = (float) Math.pow(percent, gEmphasis);
        float bPercent = (float) Math.pow(percent, bEmphasis);

        // Create the actual color component values
        int red   = (int)(r0 + rPercent*(r1-r0));
        int green = (int)(g0 + gPercent*(g1-g0));
        int blue  = (int)(b0 + bPercent*(b1-b0));

        // Fill the palette's three component arrays
        rArray[i] = (byte) red;
        gArray[i] = (byte) green;
        bArray[i] = (byte) blue;
}

// Create a palette, represented as a Java IndexColorModel object.
// We specify that the model is 8 bits deep, with 256 values for
// red, green, and blue, and that these values are obtained from the
// three arrays we just created.
myPalette = new IndexColorModel(8,  256,  rArray,  gArray,  bArray);
}
```

The last part of the initialization calls for the creation of the `Particle` objects, which will be used in the DLA algorithm. We first compute how many particles we should make, as a function of the overall area of the pixel display: generally, larger rasters need to be populated by more particles. Applets whose widths and heights are roughly a few hundred pixels will require somewhere between 20,000 to 100,000 of these invisible `Particle` objects.

```
void initializeSimulation(){
        // I determined empirically that the applet works well when there
        // are approximately 0.1 Particles per pixel. Note that larger applets
        // will have simulations which are correspondingly slower to compute.
        float particlesPerPixel = 0.1f;
        numberOfParticles = (int)(numberOfRasterPixels * particlesPerPixel);

        // Construct the array containing the Particles.
        particleArray = new Particle[numberOfParticles];
        for (int i=0; i<numberOfParticles; i++){
                particleArray[i] = new Particle();
        }
}
```

This is a sensible place to include the definition of the `Particle` object. Although these particles are a class in their own right, I've included their definition within the Dendron code, as a so-called inner class, in order to avoid the complexity of dealing with another Java file. Each particle is defined by a two-dimensional position and velocity, and offers a method by which the particle can be reset and updated.

```
private class Particle {

        // movement interpolation constants enable
        // the particle to move in a smooth way.
        static final float A = 0.9f;
        static final float B = 1.0f - A;

        float   px, py;         // Particle position
        float   vx, vy;         // Particle velocity
        float   dx, dy;         // Handy offsets
        boolean active;

        // the Particle constructor method
        public Particle(){ reset(); }
```

```
void reset(){
    // Resets the Particle to a new random location and a zero velocity.
    px = (float) (Math.random() * (float) rasterWidth);
    py = (float) (Math.random() * (float) rasterHeight);
    vx = 0;
    vy = 0;
}

void update(){
    // This method advances a Particle to its next
    // location, based on its current velocity, and
    // also evolves the Particle's velocity somewhat
    // in order to produce a smoothed-out drunk walk.

    // Coarsely integrate the current velocity
    // in order to update the Particle's position.
    px += vx;
    py += vy;

    // Do a bounds check to make sure that the Particle
    // stays within the bounds of the raster area.
    if (px > rasterWidth)  { px -= rasterWidth; }
    else if (px < 0      ) { px += rasterWidth; }
    if (py > rasterHeight) { py -= rasterHeight; }
    else if (py < 0      ) { py += rasterHeight; }

    // Compute a random deflection for the Particle.
    dx = (float)(Math.random()-0.5)*maxParticleVelocity;
    dy = (float)(Math.random()-0.5)*maxParticleVelocity;

    // Modify the velocity by that deflection,
    // smoothing it as we go with the factors A and B.
    vx = A*vx + B*dx;
    vy = A*vy + B*dy;
}
}
```

Returning now to our original Dendron class, we include some functions that can quickly restore our applet to its original (startup) condition.

The `clearRaster` method wipes the pixel array clean, while the `resetParticles` method restores the group of Particles to their original, randomly-distributed state. These methods are called whenever the user wants to clear the screen, which we implement (later) as the result of a key press.

```
    void clearRaster(){
            for (int i=0; i<numberOfRasterPixels; i++){
rasterPixels[i] = (byte) 0;
}
    }

    void resetParticles(){
            for (int i=0; i<numberOfParticles; i++){
                    particleArray[i].reset();
            }
    }
```

We now include some boilerplate applet code: some of the various kinds of extremely standard functions which are a necessary part of nearly every animated interactive applet. Here, we implement the methods to start, stop, destroy, and update the applet. The browser software calls these procedures automatically when it loads or closes your applet, so there is no reason for you to call them yourself.

```
    public void start(){
            stopAnimationThread = false;
            requestFocus();
            if (animationThread == null){
                    animationThread = new Thread (this);
                    animationThread.start();
            }
    }

    public void stop(){
            stopAnimationThread = true;
            if (animationThread != null){
                    animationThread.stop();
                    animationThread = null;
            }
    }

    public void destroy(){;}
    public void update(Graphics g) { paint(g);}
    public void update(){ paint(this.getGraphics());}
```

Earlier I mentioned that the Dendron applet is runnable. This means that it implements a method called run which executes the applet's main loop. Think of run as the motor which keeps the entire car humming. The run method is set into activity when the applet is first started.

Afterwards, for as long as the Dendron applet is active, the implementation of `run` you see here will update the DLA simulation, refresh the graphic display, and then relinquish control of the computer's CPU (with `Thread.sleep`) until it is time to execute the loop again.

To achieve animation coherent with our persistence of vision, `run` will attempt to do this every 25 milliseconds or so, giving us (optimally) a frame rate of about 50 frames per second. `run` is called automatically by the applet's thread – you shouldn't call it yourself, and you can't change its name.

```java
public void run(){
        while (animationThread != null) {

                // This is the call which updates
                // the simulation's data structures
                computeSimulation();

                // This is the call which updates the
                // display, to reflect those changes.
                update();

                        // This block of code puts the Thread to sleep for a
                        // little while in order to establish the animation's
                // frame rate, and also to free up the CPU so that it
                // can devote some cycles to its other tasks. This block
                // also handles the Thread termination, in case the user
                // leaves the applet's browser page.
                try {
                        if (!stopAnimationThread) {
                                try {Thread.sleep(threadSleepTime);}
                                catch(InterruptedException e){;}
                        } else {
                                if (animationThread != null) {
                                        animationThread.stop();
                                        animationThread = null;
                                        break;
                                }
                        }
                } catch (Exception e) { break;}
        }
}
```

Here's another important piece, the `paint` method, which is called indirectly by `run`. `paint` is the applet's main drawing method: it renders the latest raster image to the screen at every frame of animation.

Notice that we accomplish double-buffering (and thus flicker-free animation) by drawing the raster image into an Image object called `appletImage`, and then rendering the `appletImage` to the display device. If we had bypassed this step, and simply rendered the `rasterImage` into the main graphics context (single-buffering), our applet could flicker in an annoying way. Other environments like DBN and Director implement double-buffering on your behalf, but here we have to create it for ourselves.

```java
public synchronized void paint(Graphics g) {
        try
{ // This is where images are swapped, to do double-buffering.
                Graphics myGraphicsContext = appletImage.getGraphics();
                myGraphicsContext.drawImage(rasterImage, 0, 0, this);
                g.drawImage(appletImage, 0, 0, this);
        } catch (NullPointerException e) {
                // This catches possble errors.
                System.out.println("error: " + e.getMessage());
        }
}
```

Finally all of our preparations are made, and we can dive into the most interesting part of the Dendron code!

The heart of the matter

We first define a helpful pair of methods for getting and setting the individual data bytes in the `rasterPixels` array. Because the `rasterPixels` are stored in a linear array (as opposed to a two-dimensional array), we need to first do a little math to determine the actual index of the pixel we care about.

```java
int getPixel (int x, int y){
        int loc = y*rasterWidth + x;
        return (UNSIGN & rasterPixels[loc]);
}

void setPixel (int x, int y, byte b){
        int loc = y*rasterWidth + x;
        rasterPixels[loc] = b;
}
```

The next procedure, computeSimulation is the heart of
the DLA simulation itself. In it, each of the hundred
thousand or so Particles in the particleArray is made
to move across the underlying field of pixels. As each
Particle does its drunken walk across the raster, it checks
the sum of the pixel values in its local 3-by-3
neighborhood – all the pixels directly surrounding it. If
this sum is greater than the aggregationThreshold
constant, the particle assumes that it has encountered a
part of the structure. At this point, it adds on to the
structure in its location by adding the constant
ACCRETE_BYTE to the value of the pixel in its location.

```
void computeSimulation(){

    for (int i=0; i<numberOfParticles; i++){
        // For every Particle in the particleArray, test it to see
        // if it neighbors a pixel that is part of the root structure.

        // Get a reference to a Particle in the array;
        // advance this Particle to its latest position,
        // and obtain its approximate integer coordinates.
        Particle P = particleArray[i];
        P.update();
        int x = (int) P.px;
        int y = (int) P.py;

        // Test to make sure that the Particle's location is within
        // the bounds of the raster array.
        if ((x > 0) && (x < (rasterWidth-1)) &&
            (y > 0) && (y < (rasterHeight-1))){

            // Fetch the values of each pixel in the
            // 3x3 neighborhood of the Particle.
            int val1 = getPixel (x-1, y-1);     // Northwest
            int val2 = getPixel (x,   y-1);     // North
            int val3 = getPixel (x+1, y-1);     // Northeast
            int val4 = getPixel (x-1, y  );     // West
            int val5 = getPixel (x,   y  );     // Center
            int val6 = getPixel (x+1, y  );     // East
            int val7 = getPixel (x-1, y+1);     // Southwest
            int val8 = getPixel (x,   y+1);     // South
            int val9 = getPixel (x+1, y+1);     // Southeast

            // The sum of these values is a good indication of whether
            // or not the Particle's pixel neighborhood is empty or full.
            int sum =     val1 + val2 + val3 +
```

```
                                      val4 + val5 + val6 +
                                      val7 + val8 + val9;

                // If the pixel neighborhood already has a sufficient amount
                // of material in it — where sufficiency is determined by the
                // aggregationThreshold — then add further to the structure
                // by brightening the pixel in the Particle's location.
                if (sum >= aggregationThreshold){

                    // To brighten the pixel, we add an incremental ACCRETE_BYTE
                    // to its old value, and then re-set the pixel with this sum.
                    int oldval = getPixel(x, y);
                    int newval = Math.min(255, oldval + ACCRETE_BYTE);
                    setPixel (x, y, (byte) newval);

                    // Since the current Particle has served its purpose, we can
                    // reset it to a new, randomly chosen location.
                                      P.reset();
                }
            }
        }

        // Now we've finished modifying rasterPixels for the time being.
        // The next line is special; it causes the MemoryImageSource myMIS
        // to pipe all of the recently-updated pixels from the rasterPixels
        // array into the rasterImage Image.
        myMIS.newPixels(0, 0, rasterWidth, rasterHeight);
}
```

The version of computeSimulation above was written for maximum clarity, but was poorly optimized for speed of execution. For the sake of simplicity, it was also written to be short on distracting bells and whistles. But much of the real pleasure of interacting with Dendron is a function of the responsiveness of its simulation, and much of the richness and variety of its graphical results emerges from a few simple elaborations to its algorithm. For this reason I present a second version below, called computeSimulation2, which speeds up some computations at the same time that it adds a feature or two. To engage it, change the run method to call this version instead of the first one.

This version of the simulation has two important enhancements not present in the earlier one. The first of these is that the threshold required for a pixel to be added to the structure is made dynamic. By raising this number over time, the growth of the structure is progressively slowed! This gradual change in growth accounts for the different kinds of branch-edges in the accompanying images.

The second important enhancement in this version is the use of a progressive blurring technique. Whenever a particle adds to the structure of the aggregate pixel colony, it also (very slightly) blurs its neighborhood of pixels, with a call to the `blurNeighborhood` function. This has the effect of distributing a small portion of its accretion-material to a wider area. This small change feeds back into the DLA algorithm, producing powerful differences in the structure's overall appearance.

```
private void computeSimulation2(){
    // An optimized version of computeSimulation() with some extra features:
    // − The aggregation threshold is made dynamic;
    // − A progressive blurring is added to the process of deposition;
    // − Pointer math is used to speed our evaluation of the neighborhood.

    // Slow the growth over time by raising the aggregation threshold.
    aggregationThreshold+=0.15f;

    Particle P;
    int sum;
    int x, y, loc;
    int locc, locn, locs;

    final int minX = 1;
    final int minY = 1;
    final int maxX = rasterWidth-2;
    final int maxY = rasterHeight-2;

    int count = 0;
    for (int i=0; i<numberOfParticles; i++){
        P = particleArray[i];
        x = (int) P.px;
        y = (int) P.py;
        P.update();

        if ((x > minX) && (x < maxX) &&
            (y > minY) && (y < maxY)){
            loc = y*rasterWidth + x;
            locc = loc - 1;
            locn = locc - rasterWidth;
```

```
                locs = locc + rasterWidth;

                // Use pointer math to optimize the collection of the
                // neighboring pixel values.
                sum     = (UNSIGN & rasterPixels [locn++]) +
                          (UNSIGN & rasterPixels [locn++]) +
                          (UNSIGN & rasterPixels [locn  ]) +
                          (UNSIGN & rasterPixels [locc++]) +
                          (UNSIGN & rasterPixels [locc++]) +
                          (UNSIGN & rasterPixels [locc  ]) +
                          (UNSIGN & rasterPixels [locs++]) +
                          (UNSIGN & rasterPixels [locs++]) +
                          (UNSIGN & rasterPixels [locs  ]);

            if (sum >= aggregationThreshold){
                    rasterPixels[loc] = (byte) Math.min(255,
                                  UNSIGN & rasterPixels[loc])+ACCRETE_BYTE);
                    if ((count++)%blurFrequency == 0){ blurNeighborhood(loc);}
                    P.reset();
            }
        }
    }
        myMIS.newPixels(0, 0, rasterWidth, rasterHeight);
    }
```

The `blurNeighborhood` function below, called by `computeSimulation2` smudges the 3-by-3 neighborhood of pixels centered around a given index in the `rasterPixels` array. We blur the pixels of the 3-by-3 region in a certain order – from the center towards the edges – in order to minimize any asymmetric blurring effects. The `blurNeighborhood` function uses a subsequently-defined subroutine, `blur`, to perform all of its actual pixel modifications.

```
    void blurNeighborhood (int locC){
// Blur the neighborhood of pixels around a central location.

// First check to make sure that our location is within
// appropriate and legal bounds.
if ((locC >= (rasterWidth+1)) &&
            (locC < (numberOfRasterPixels - rasterWidth -1))){

                // Define the indices of the North (upper)
                // and South (lower) neighboring pixels.
                int locN = locC - rasterWidth;
                int locS = locC + rasterWidth;
```

```
            // Blur the center pixel first
            blur(locC);

            // Now blur the north, south, west and east pixels
            blur(locN  );
            blur(locS  );
            blur(locC-1);
            blur(locC+1);

            // Finally, blur the corner pixels: NW, NE, SW, SE.
            blur(locN-1);
            blur(locN+1);
            blur(locS-1);
            blur(locS+1);
        }
    }
```

The next function, `blur`, reassigns the brightness of a pixel to be a weighted average of itself with the pixels in the 3x3 neighborhood around it. If its surrounding neighbors are darker, it will become darker; if its neighbors are lighter, it will become lighter.

The algorithm used here, called Gaussian blurring, is a subset of a much wider range of powerful signal processing techniques called convolution filtering. Convolution filtering works by reassigning a pixel's value to be a function of the pixels around it. So, for example, if each of the pixels in an image is re-assigned to be the average of its neighbors, we achieve a blurring effect. On the other hand, if each pixel is reassigned to be more different from its neighbors, we effectively sharpen the image. Convolution filtering is an important topic in electrical engineering and computer science, and many dozens of unnecessarily abstruse books have been written on the topic.

```
    void blur (int locC){
        // Blur the value of a pixel at index locC in the rasterPixels array.

        // First, we'll do a check to make sure that we can blur this pixel.
        // We'll hit problems if the pixel's upper or lower neighbors lie
        // outside the bounds of the rasterPixels array.
        if ((locC >= rasterWidth) &&
            (locC < (numberOfRasterPixels - rasterWidth))){
                // We compute the array indices of the neighbors in our 3x3
                // region, numbering them from 1 through 9 as follows:
```

```
                      // 1  2  3
                      // 4  5  6
                      // 7  8  9
        int loc1 = locC - rasterWidth - 1;          // Northwest
        int loc2 = locC - rasterWidth;              // North
        int loc3 = locC - rasterWidth + 1;          // Northeast
        int loc4 = locC - 1;                        // West
        int loc5 = locC;                            // Center
        int loc6 = locC + 1;                        // East
        int loc7 = locC + rasterWidth - 1;          // Southwest
        int loc8 = locC + rasterWidth;              // South
        int loc9 = locC + rasterWidth + 1;          // Southeast

        // Now we fetch the values of the nine pixels out of the
        // rasterPixels byte array. We need to do some unaesthetic
        // bitwise math with the UNSIGN constant in order to extract
        // the bytes as unsigned integers (from 0...255). Otherwise Java
               // will (by default) cast bytes to signed integers (-128...127).
        int val1 = UNSIGN & rasterPixels[loc1];
        int val2 = UNSIGN & rasterPixels[loc2];
        int val3 = UNSIGN & rasterPixels[loc3];
        int val4 = UNSIGN & rasterPixels[loc4];
        int val5 = UNSIGN & rasterPixels[loc5];
        int val6 = UNSIGN & rasterPixels[loc6];
        int val7 = UNSIGN & rasterPixels[loc7];
        int val8 = UNSIGN & rasterPixels[loc8];
        int val9 = UNSIGN & rasterPixels[loc9];

        // Now we use a 3x3 Gaussian blurring convolution kernel
        // to determine the weighted average of the pixels. This kernel has
        // the following multiplicative weights assigned to each location:
        // 1  2  1
        // 2  4  2
        // 1  2  1

        int sum = (    1*val1 + 2*val2 + 1*val3 +
                       2*val4 + 4*val5 + 2*val6 +
                       1*val7 + 2*val8 + 1*val9 );

        int weightedAverage = sum/16;

        rasterPixels[locC] = (byte)(weightedAverage);
    }
}
```

All that remains are the methods that handle the user's interactions with the applet. Chief among these is the createLine function, which draws a line of pixels in the rasterPixels array in the location where the user has dragged the cursor. This is a simple task, but the implementation presented here is not very efficient at all – for a faster technique, please investigate the excellent algorithm developed by Bresenham, which can be found at http://www.cs.helsinki.fi/group/goa/mallinnus/lines/bresenh.html

```
void createLine (int x0, int y0, int x1, int y1){
        // This method takes the x- and y-coordinates of two points,
        // and draws a line between them (in the raster of pixels)
        // by depositing the DRAW_BYTE value into the rasterPixels array.

        float dx = x1-x0;
        float dy = y1-y0;
        float dh = (float)(Math.sqrt(dx*dx + dy*dy));

        int x, y;
        int ym, xm, index;
        float percent;

        for (int i=0; i<dh; i++){
                percent = (float)i/dh;
                x = (int)(x0 + percent*dx);
                y = (int)(y0 + percent*dy);

                ym = y%rasterHeight;
                xm = x%rasterWidth;
                index = ym*rasterWidth +xm;
                rasterPixels[index] = DRAW_BYTE;
        }
}
```

Finally we present the built-in interaction methods provided by Java's Applet class. I've chosen to use the older Java 1.1 event handlers – mouseDown, mouseDrag, mouseUp, mouseMove, and keyDown – instead of using the newer Listener-based technique, as I've had fewer problems with them in practice and I think they're simpler to understand. There are a couple of details worth noting: one is that both mouseDown and mouseDrag call createLine, allowing the user to draw. Another is that, as shown below, mouseDown resets the aggregationThreshold to 1; this is an optional nicety for particular use with the fancier computeSimulation2 method.

Finally, note that the `keyDown` handler allows the user some interactive control of the simulation's performance, by permitting keyboard-based manipulation of the `aggregationThreshold`. Other system constants could certainly be stubbed out here as well. Perhaps the most important key handler is that for the space bar, which is assigned to clearing the screen and allows us to start a new drawing!

```
// interaction methods
public boolean mouseDown (Event evt, int x, int y){
        aggregationThreshold = 1;
        prevMouseX = mouseX;
        prevMouseY = mouseY;
        mouseX = x;
        mouseY = y;
        createLine  (prevMouseX, prevMouseY, mouseX, mouseY);
        return true;
}

public boolean mouseDrag (Event evt, int x, int y){
        prevMouseX = mouseX;
        prevMouseY = mouseY;
        mouseX = x;
        mouseY = y;
        createLine  (prevMouseX, prevMouseY, mouseX, mouseY);
        return true;
}

public boolean mouseUp   (Event evt, int x, int y){
        prevMouseX = mouseX;
        prevMouseY = mouseY;
        mouseX = x;
        mouseY = y;
        return true;
}

public boolean mouseMove (Event evt, int x, int y){
        prevMouseX = mouseX;
        prevMouseY = mouseY;
        mouseX = x;
        mouseY = y;
        return true;
}

public boolean keyDown(Event evt, int inputKeyInteger) {
        // Handle the key events that are sent to the applet.
```

```
        char inputCharacter = (char) inputKeyInteger;
        // Convert the input key's integer into a character.

        switch (inputCharacter){
                // Do different things depending on which key was pressed.

                case ' ':
                        // If the user pressed the space bar, then clear the pixels.
                        clearRaster();
                        resetParticles();
                        break;

                case '[':
                        aggregationThreshold = Math.max(1, aggregationThreshold - 1);
                        break;

                case ']':
                        aggregationThreshold = Math.min(255, aggregationThreshold + 1);
                        break;

        }
        return true;
    }

} // This paren closes the Dendron class definition.
```

You can see the code in action at http://www.friendsofed.com/4x4/generative/golan. Even if you do not consider yourself to be a programmer, I hope this tutorial encourages you to take an interest in the development processes behind the software tools you use, and inspires you to start along the road towards the creation of some unique interactive experiments of your own.

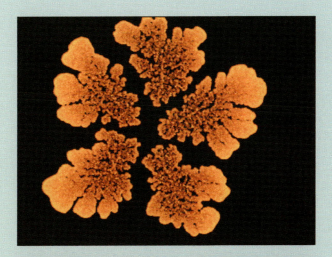

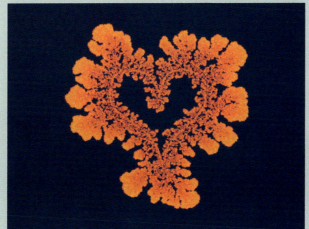

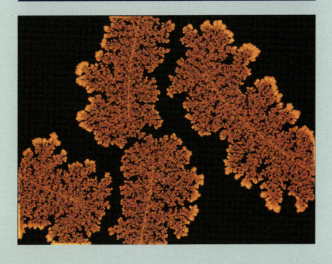

each author was invited to remix the other works submitted for the book – the following pages display the resulting hybrids

interference is a q and a session with the four authors

noise is the sound of the private discussion forum in which the authors discussed the project with each other

INTERFERENCE – SOME QUESTIONS, SOME ANSWERS, SOME WHITE NOISE

ED: WHAT ARE YOUR RESPONSES TO THE OTHER THREE ARTISTS' WORK?

golan: i'm pleased to be alongside such high-quality, thoughtfully-considered work.

lia: i guess that with any work i see there are always different levels of perception for me: the state of the used programming skills, the aesthetics, the main "principle" behind the work, the (im)possibility for me to develop something else out of it and much more. each of the pieces fulfilled my expectations in one way or the other.

meta: all are interesting at different levels and for different reasons. the writing from everyone is inspiring and enlightening – revealing how different people approach similar concepts and issues.

adrian: they made me smile. golan, lia and meta are all known for their unique and original techniques. it's quite common now for code to be re-used endlessly without proper attention being paid to the craftwork of programming. to see fresh processes applied in such a visually stimulating manner really helps alleviate the nausea caused by all this 'generative shockwave flash' stuff.

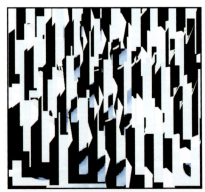

LIA vs   META

ED: HOW DID YOU APPROACH THE MECHANICAL RECLAMATION PART OF THIS PROJECT?

meta: for ade and golan's pieces, i followed a similar methodology. first i created an image with their works & took a screenshot of it. second i imported these images into the application that i made for the book and used it to create the new images. for lia's piece, i actually altered the work itself in director. there are three screenshots and two director files.

META vs GOLAN

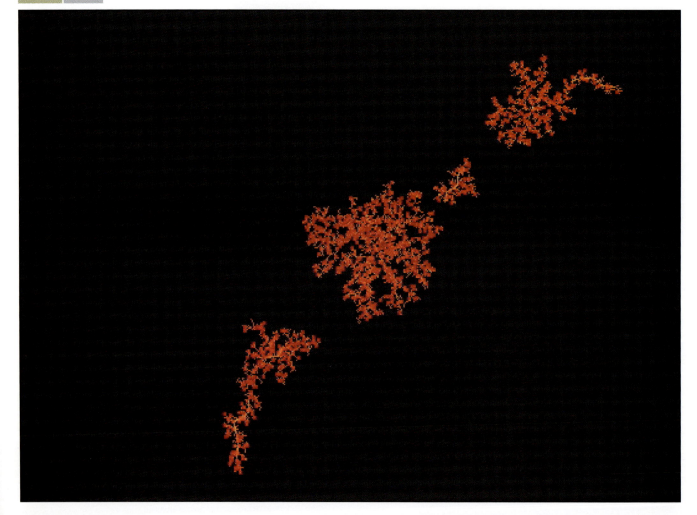

META vs ADRIAN

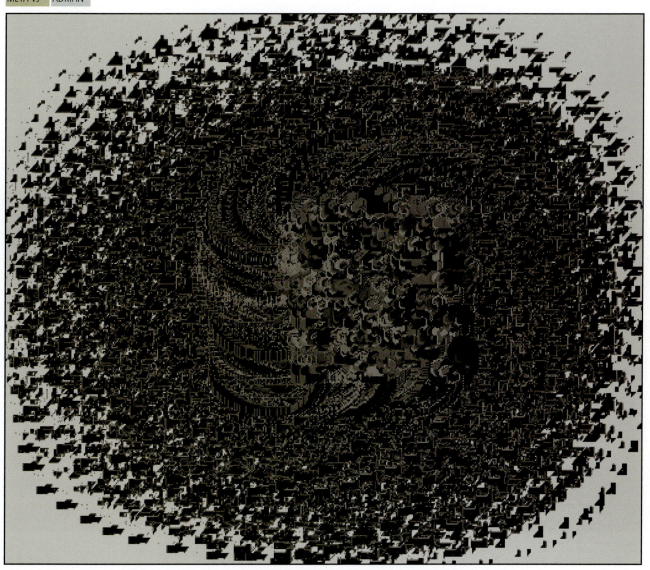

META vs LIA

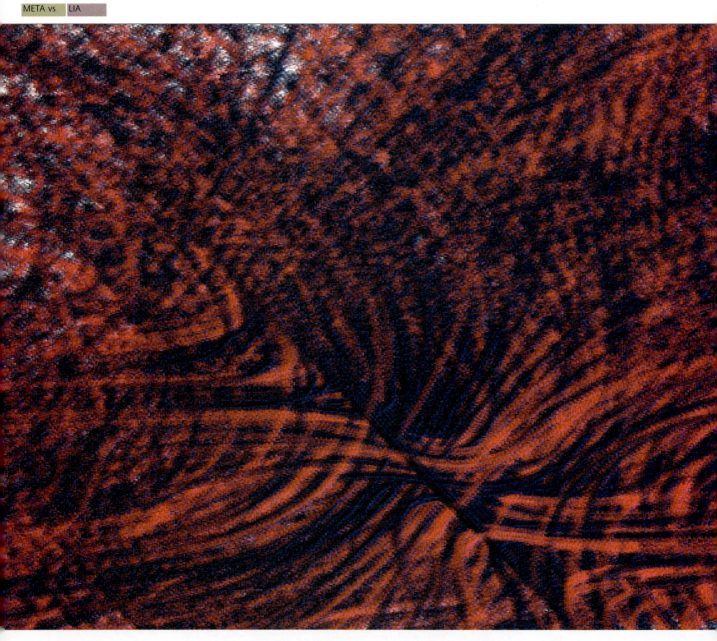

META vs LIA

lia: i think i will go through my experiences with the other authors' pieces one by one – as i got the chance to see them and play around with them.

meta's piece – i immediately decided not to try to fiddle around with max, because i already gave it a try a long time ago and didn't find myself too comfortable in this programming environment. i have to admit that in the beginning i was trying to "redo" the nice pictures i knew from meta's web page – using the tool he provided us with. but after i while i found myself liking it more, not using all the implemented features together and keeping it all rather simple: just moving around a movie without a 3d-source. and with that i had quite a lot of fun.

so in the case of the application of meta i was just "using" it, extending, mutating or transforming the idea behind it in any way: just being a happy user. i thought about the possibility of re-doing something in director which would give similar results, but then i knew immediately that this would be no fun at all – because this would mean just to copy the idea behind the application out of one programming environment into another.

ade's piece – it was quite nice to have some immediate working results when going through ade's tutorial step by step. for me it is very inspiring to permanently have some visible feedback when i'm developing code to see what exactly is possible and what not. of course i'm also in this case lacking knowledge of the programming language itself, so all i did was more or less use the readymade code that ade provided us with in the tutorial and redo some things with more or less the same command lines just in another order. i very much like the fact that this program works with vector graphics, which means the results produced with it are not so much bound to the screen like pieces made with director.

golan's piece – i very much like the idea of producing something which is normally "done by nature" (like the growth of mushrooms) through mathematics. i have to admit that i'm not into java at all, so, after i had a quick look at the code i was rather scared away from trying to redo this piece in a modified way.

LIA vs META

LIA vs ADRIAN

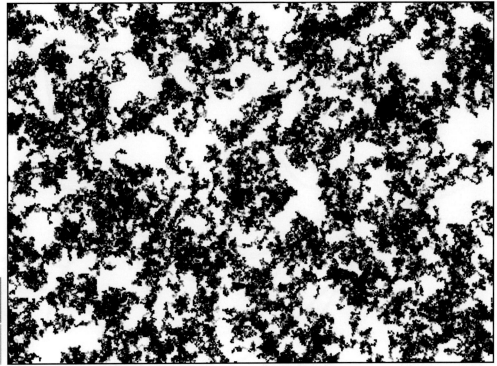

LIA vs GOLAN

golan: i've been a big fan of lia's work for several years and i was excited to be on a project with her. i would have liked to remix the pieces by ade and meta as well, but i wasn't able to get a copy of visual basic in time for the book deadline, and i'm afraid my only macintosh (a iici) is a bit too slow to run meta's nato work.

here in the states we have a toy similar to the one lia was inspired by for her project. the american version is called "spirograph"... it's the same thing really. i used to have one when i was a kid. the shapes it makes are called epicycloids and hypocycloids.

i made some small changes to lia's tutorial piece by having the center of the epicycloid system follow the cursor around. i also measured the cursor velocity and used that computation to drive some of the inner parameters of lia's math, such as her angular velocity constant. it's been a long time since i used director and i'm also impressed with how well the environment has developed. truthfully, i haven't had this much fun in weeks.

GOLAN vs LIA

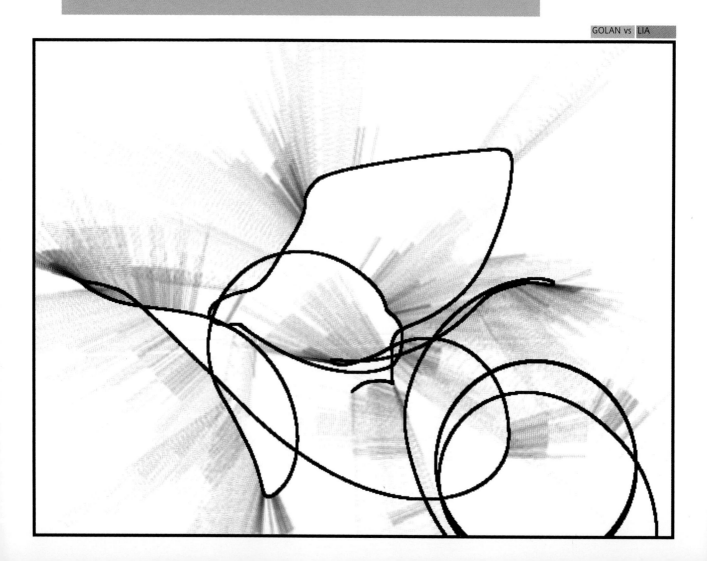

adrian: immediately we all came to the conclusion that this was going to be hard, because each of us has our own working process, and we all use different technologies in very different ways. apart from the steep learning curve involved with learning a new programming environment, one of the hardest things about programming is when you have to take someone else's code and modify it for yourself.

i've always been inspired by applying an abstract and alien working process to what would otherwise be quite a straightforward process. it seemed natural to want to do the same here, although i hadn't figured out quite how to achieve that until i received the files from the other authors.

as soon as i took a look at them i realized that my computer wasn't initially set up to use them: golan's java applet locked up my browser (it's not his fault: it happens all the time), lia's dir file was useless to me as i don't own director, and meta's compiled max runtime hadn't downloaded properly, and i was left with an unknown "document" which i couldn't execute because my mac hadn't picked up the resource fork (or some other similarly obscure problem).

so i had a bundle of useless files. initially i would have just taken the steps required to get the files running: re-install my java vm, go use a computer with director installed, re-download the max runtime.

but instead i hooked onto the idea of files being useless because the computer didn't or couldn't understand or make sense of them. when that happens on a macintosh you just end up with a default blank file, with no icon, and the type is just described as "document". it's less common on a pc, although it does happen sometimes. but these files *did* contain data, regardless of the fact that my computer couldn't do anything with them.

so i set about writing a utility that would use the "meaningless" data in the files to generate auto-illustrator plug-ins. the result was the auto-coder wizard, a humorous little application that allows you to generate a valid xeo auto-illustrator plug-in from any file on your hard disk.

the actual translation from binary data to auto-illustrator plug-in is arbitrary. certain bits from certain bytes of the "source file" are translated into commands and numbers in a purely arbitrary form. as the programmer of auto-coder, i decided exactly what those translations would be.

yet it's not possible to know exactly what the plug-in will do once it has been generated. the plug-in code created is so abstractly removed from the actual original data that, actually, the plug-in could do anything. and "anything" includes "nothing", too. during the testing phase of writing auto-coder, i produced so many auto-illustrator plug-ins that although they contain lots of valid code, when run, they didn't actually do anything.

so what i'm facilitating here is not just a translation from one abstract form into another, but a transformation because part of that translation process is in the construction of a code, that in turn generates some form of output (hopefully).

auto-coder doesn't facilitate any sort of collaboration, although what it does do is apply – in purely conceptual terms only – a form of reinterpretation of an original work using personal, subjective, and wholly arbitrary decisions which cannot be rationalized. i would say that that is how any form of interpretation occurs, usually it is far less abstracted.

the second designer looks at the work of the first, and applies arbitrary decisions and working processes in order to achieve something that possibly resembles the original work, although more importantly carries clear signals that the new work carries the new designer's hallmark.

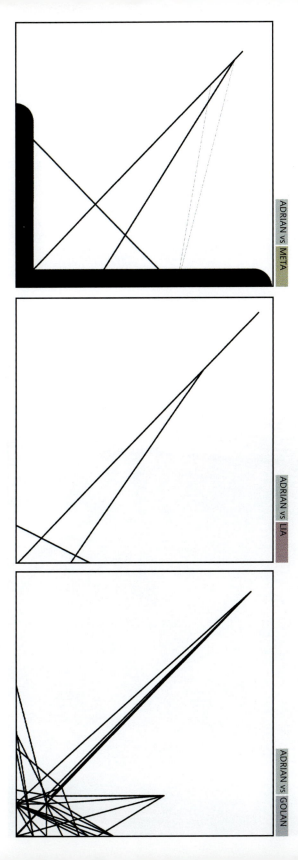

ADRIAN vs META

ADRIAN vs LIA

ADRIAN vs GOLAN

ED: THE THEME *LIFE & OBLIVION* IS VERY WIDE. DO YOU GET ANY SENSE OF THAT THEME IN THE WORKS YOU'VE SEEN?

lia: for me the term "life" at the same time includes the term "oblivion": everything in life can fall into oblivion again (which happens with most of the things i guess). when working with code some parts are further developed and "grown" into something new, and some parts are just skipped in this further development.

meta: the key word is "life". there is an element of life processes to all of the works presented. they are interactive. reactive. evolving.

META vs LIA

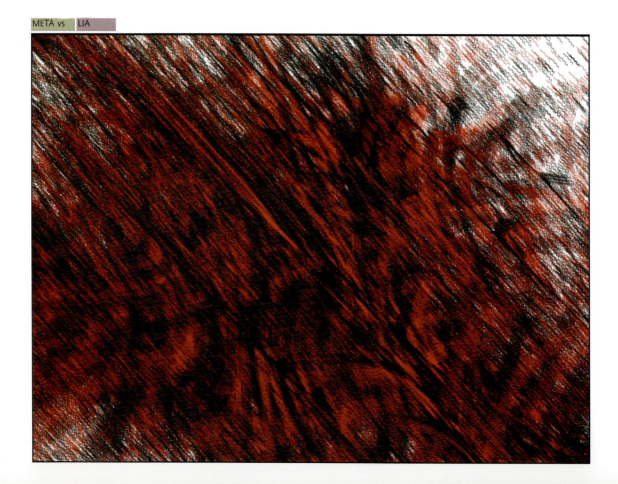

golan: i think the really important thing is that the four different pieces give a really good spread of different takes on the idea of generativity.

adrian: it's not right to compare our works like that – we're all so different and our work reflects that diversity (and not just in a technical sense, either). i was going to say something about my lack of design skills here but in a way i don't feel like comparing final results – it's a needless diversion. we're not really doing this to create fixed objects – we're all doing this to explore the wealth of possibilities that code makes available to us.

meta: this question implies a sort of competition and that was not the case here. we all approached a similar concept from different directions.

'A vs   GOLAN

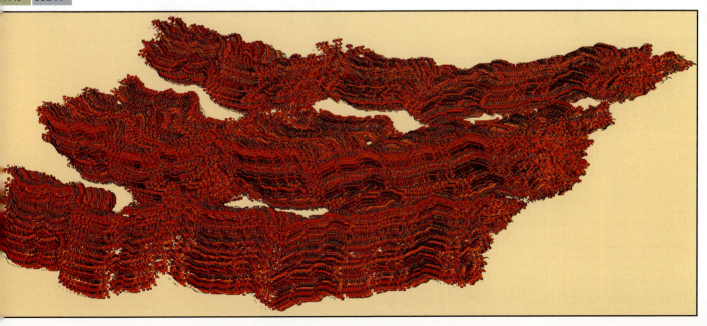

ED: YOU ALL USE DIFFERENT LANGUAGES AND TECHNIQUES. IS THERE ANYTHING IN THE TECHNICAL MAKE-UP OF THE OTHER PIECES THAT SURPRISES OR INTRIGUES YOU?

golan: technology rarely surprises me – except for that physicist recently who did some crazy stuff with neutrino teleportation. the thing about the others' works which gives a surprising feeling, is the freshness of their concepts combined with their high-quality execution.

lia: the less i know about a programming language, the more i wonder how this could be done.

meta: the ease of authoring for adrian's auto-illustrator plug-ins is intriguing. the fact that the plug-ins are simple text files is quite good. all applications should be so open. html is a language that is incredibly robust by design. you can insert a great deal of noise into an html document, random characters, malformed tags, and such like. and yet, *something* will still display. errors usually do not cause everything to come to a screeching halt but rather are incorporated into the page somehow.

it would be nice if all applications would accept external modification in this manner, perhaps in the form of plug-ins. adrian's auto-coder program begins to approach this idea.

adrian: what is "technical make-up"? make-up is something you apply later to mask over the blemishes. i'm more interested in the flesh and bones here. but then, asking whether i thought the technical flesh and bones of the other pieces surprised me seems silly too.

META vs GOLAN

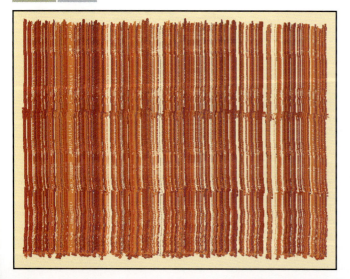

ED: DO YOU THINK THAT IN THE FUTURE MORE ARTISTS AND DESIGNERS WILL BECOME INTERESTED IN CODE AND PROGRAMMING IN ORDER TO TAKE CONTROL OF THEIR CREATIVE PROCESSES? OR DO YOU THINK THIS WILL REMAIN AN ACTIVITY AT THE MARGINS, WITH COMPANIES LIKE MACROMEDIA AND ADOBE EXTENDING THEIR DOMINATION?

golan: widespread coding is inevitable, but people will not be aware that what they are doing is programming.

lia: i guess that to have the patience to create their own drawing tool someone has to be interested in both programming and aesthetics. i don't think at all that there has to be a difference in the quality of works produced, depending on if they are done with some traditional programs or with something home-made – because that way of thinking would lead to the (wrong) statement that someone can only do as good works as the programs they use.

meta: more artists & designers *are* becoming interested in code and programming. but this is a very small niche, and will remain so for quite some time.

the basic limiting factor is that all forms of programming have their own learning curve. some are steeper than others, yet all are *much* steeper than the curve involved in learning an application like photoshop or flash. there is also a temperament, a mindset involved in programming that can be quite at odds with the one required for creative work and artistic expression.

i find programming languages like lingo or java or c++ to be too abstract and do not enjoy working with them. personally, i dislike math and always have – but i dislike restrictions on my creativity even more. i work in max because it provides a graphical interface to the abstractions of code. it combines the power and flexibility of custom coding with the ease of use of a well-designed and simple graphical interface.

at the same time, it is not required that one code their own custom solutions in order to produce excellent work. limitation can lead to innovation.

adrian: it's critical to the progression of art that programming is not seen as a science. artists can code too. it really bugs me when i see artists hiring programmers to do the dirty work because, for me, the crucial part of the creative process is embedded within the act of programming. and programming is becoming a very vague thing these days anyway, so who says what is programming and what isn't? have i answered the question yet? i'm not sure i have.

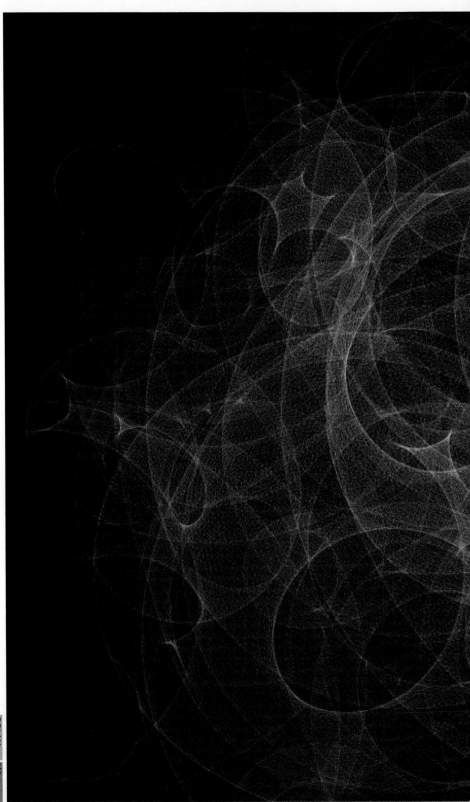

GOLAN vs LIA

ED: WHAT COLLABORATIVE PROJECTS HAVE YOU TRIED IN THE PAST? DO YOU THINK THIS ONE HAS WORKED? DOES COLLABORATION USUALLY RESULT IN A LACK OF FOCUS, OR IS THE SUM GREATER THAN ITS PARTS? IS IT A TRAUMATIC OR EMPHATIC PROCESS?

adrian: in what way did we collaborate?

golan: collaboration is complex and difficult. i've had successful collaborations that produced lousy work, and horrible collaborations that produced incredible work, but no-one could ever speak to each other ever again. it's a cauldron.

lia: collaborating in a project in general means an exchange of brain-contents and therefore most of the time it's fun. in the case of the book i didn't feel too much that i was really "collaborating" with someone – besides the part of trying to "remix" each others pieces. because all of us were mainly working on our pieces without having too much exchange of ideas or some influence on each other before that.

meta: this did not seem like a true collaborative process to me. there was reacting and interpreting, but for this to have been a truly collaborative effort there would have to have been more stages of action and reaction over a longer period of time and at a more basic level.

ED: DO YOU HAVE AN AWARENESS OF, OR AN INTEREST IN, AN AUDIENCE FOR YOUR WORK? ARE YOU CREATING WORK FOR YOURSELF PRIMARILY, OR ARE YOU CONTRIBUTING TO SOME WIDER DISCOURSE ON ART AND TECHNOLOGY?

golan: hmm. i create work primarily for myself, within a wider discourse on art and technology. no really, i do.

lia: of course i like the interest of an audience – otherwise i would not make my works available for anyone else, but at the same time i'm mainly working for my own pleasure. all in all i don't have any particular reason to do my works. i just like playing around.

adrian: mmm now that's a tricky one. personally, i do my work for selfish reasons – it's a form of expression that doesn't really pander to any particular audience other than myself. it always surprises me when people like what i do because, to be honest, i don't really do it for them. i do it for myself. i guess that sounds a bit arrogant, but then if i didn't do that then my entire theory based upon self-expression would fall apart.

there is an element of entertainment in what i do, in the form of parody, although it's to critique certain existing systems and not just to give the audience a laugh – that's not really something i've explored in this book, apart from with the auto-coder wizard.

meta: it is interesting to hear other peoples' interpretations of and reaction to what i do. at the same time it is important not to become overly concerned with this, otherwise one ends up following a carrot on a stick straight into a wall.

am i creating work for myself primarily, or contributing to some wider discourse on art and technology? i am interested in exploring and discovering.

ED: DO YOU KNOW IN WHAT DIRECTION YOU ARE HEADED IN THE FUTURE? ARE THERE NEW AREAS THAT YOU ARE KEEN TO EXPLORE?

meta: shhhhh.

adrian: we'll see.

lia: i have no idea what will catch my attention or will inspire me in the future. if i knew it already, this would not be in the future, no?

golan: mechatronics and music.

META vs

LIA

ED: IF YOU HAD LIMITLESS RESOURCES WHAT TYPE OF SOFTWARE/HARDWARE WOULD YOU CREATE? WHAT CONSTRAINTS LIMIT YOU IN YOUR CURRENT WORK?

adrian: no, i think you've missed the point: if you can make software, then you do have (virtually) limitless resources at your hands. you can do anything with software. i mean it.

golan: i'm interested in working with physical media now – using lasers to draw things – it's hard to explain. limitless resources would mean people and time, not hardware or software.

lia: this question reminds me of the genie which gives you a free wish. in this sense: i would like to have a special hardware with a special software running on there which allows me to have a continuing process of learning and exploring new stuff with a lot of fun. the most constraining thing with my work i guess is me: because i just simply don't know how to do many many things – but at the same time i would not see it as "my" work anymore if i would ask someone else to do this or that for me.

meta: for the software, i'd like an environment that rendered operating systems, software and hardware, and file formats irrelevant – something that translated all types of media from one to another in realtime with no restrictions.

what would be the result if a system were established that allowed the output of any program to be fed into the input of any other program with all file formats and types being translated from one to the other in realtime? audio files spill into text documents, appearing as words. paragraphs. metaphors.

editing a text document triggers a series of changes in an image editing program. filters are applied. layers are rearranged. hue and saturation are adjusted as lines are typed. adjusting the angles and colors of a vector-based image simultaneously adjusts the attack and decay characteristics of a software synthesizer which is playing a melody composed of midi signals derived from the contents of an email.

what new aesthetic forms would be created? discovered? how would our computing environment and habits – and by extension, our very way of life – alter in the presence of such a system?

digital synesthesia without a manual.

as for the hardware, perhaps organic computers that ran on oxygen and sunlight and upgraded themselves constantly, growing and evolving new components and capabilities.

what constraints limit me in my current work?
the need for sleep.
the need for food and water.
attention span.
lifespan.

ED: WHO WOULD HAVE BEEN YOUR THREE DREAM COLLABORATORS – LIVING OR DEAD? WHY?

golan: you mean, instead of ade, lia, and meta? that's not a fair question. i'd like to live in paris in the 1920s or new york city in the 70s but that's not possible. i was lucky to be at the acg in the 90s. i think one can always find great collaborators if one looks, though.

lia: anyone is welcome as a collaborator, as long as there is something inspiring going on.

meta: unknown. it is best to remain open to various possibilities. john cage with a computer science degree would be interesting, though.

adrian: golan, lia and meta.

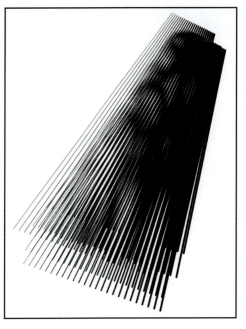

LIA vs ADRIAN

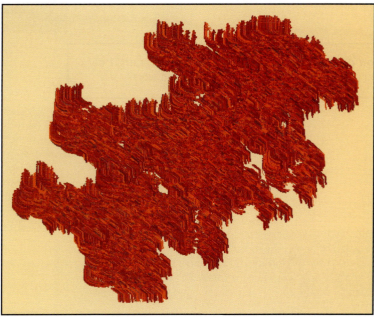

META vs GOLAN

NOISE – random excerpts and final words from the post book discussion

ED: how have you found the experience of collating your materials and submitting them for publication? do you find it's relevant to what you want to do? how would you change it?

adrian: personally i find it quite hard to put into words exactly what my work is about, especially if i'm asked to give technical details. although i'm fascinated and driven by technology, i'm never that interested in talking in a "how to" style. what you have to promote is the individual's sense of exploration that will spark their own learning adventure, rather than just lending them yours.

golan: i'm the opposite way. whenever I talk, it's always a lecture. i'm the most didactic and pedantic person i know. well I'm sort of kidding. but actually i found it quite natural to write in this style.

ED: lia, how did the recent concert go (http://www.at-c.org)? does it help you progress when you do such commission work?

lia: the work i do for @c is not really a commission work, but it's an ongoing process: the longer i make the live-visuals for the concerts, the more we can really work "together" – that means that the musicians also can influence the creation of the visuals through the sound they are producing, and i get to know better in which way they are used to let the music evolve, so that i can already "expect" the next direction of the sounds.

golan: that @c site is brill. as far as my own commission work, i try to convince other people to commission me to make things I wanted to make in the first place. then i enjoy what i do. but sometimes i don't get so lucky.

LIA vs ADRIAN

GOLAN vs LIA

ADRIAN vs META

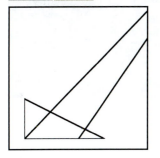

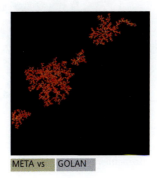

META vs GOLAN

golan: wow, lia how did you do this?!?!? it's great! did you re-implement my tutorial in director, or mess with the java?

lia: i was not really having a too close look at the java-code, because i would not have understood too much of it anyway: so i did something rather simple and quick in director – only re-using the main "principle" golan is talking about in the first part of his tutorial.

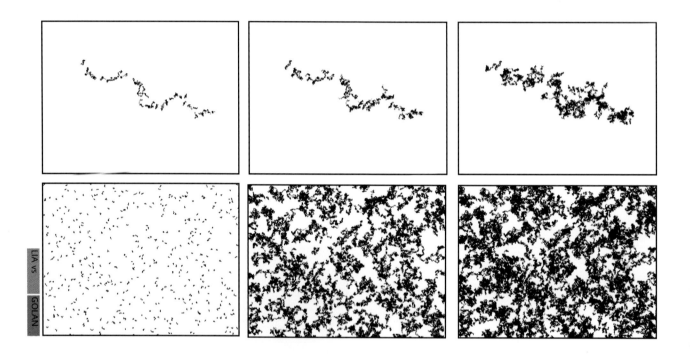

LIA vs GOLAN

ED: what do you hope is the point of the book? does it have one for you? what do you want it to do/achieve/be?

adrian: i feel that the point is to really demonstrate how worthwhile programming is as a way of extending your creativity. for me it's not so much about showing how to do things specifically, but to demonstrate that you can, and to inspire people to pick up some tools for themselves and discover what it's like to write your first computer program – without being blindly led by the hand.

lia: the maybe-use of this book – in general i hope that the book is showing people what *can* be done to produce graphical results with different programming languages. it doesn't necessarily have to be one of the ones used in the book of course – it could also be plain html, to start with (like i did).

i don't like too much the idea of people just "re-using" the codes provided in the book simply as they are – without changing/improving/mutating/transforming/hacking them in their own way for their own use.

i still have this trauma with this flash script where some elements are following the mouse – building a line according to where the mouse has been moved previously over the screen: after the code was "set free" on the net as a seed for further modifications (as i like to see open source code) almost each and every single webpage had "elements following the mouse-movement" online. in that way the whole script (which i basically still like) was "sold out" and got boring as hell. it has just been replicated too many times without any attempt to really "use" it in the sense of improving it (a few weeks later the same thing happened with a nice "rotating-cube" flash-script).

so i really hope to see something NEW coming out of the use of this book!

i like very much the changing/improvements that golan did with my piece: even if he may have "used" my script as a starting point, he did something new and back-inspiring for me!

i don't really see the pictures i created with meta's application for instance as my own creation – i can't be too proud of them, because the main work was done by meta. and the same thing is valid for ade's piece: without the whole environment he already programmed, the few lines of code i tried out there would not work at all.

adrian – if i could jump in here and emphasize lia's last point: i believe code is an extension of the self (albeit a crude and mechanic extension), so it makes sense to believe that when you interact with code, you're interacting with someone else – although it doesn't carry the same temporal and physical qualities we're all used to. i definitely treat auto-illustrator as though it were me. designers who are using my code are collaborating with me in the construction of vector designs. if i just wanted to write a vector design application, i wouldn't have bothered – there are far more professional vector design applications available that do a much better job. but the point is that code offers a new, disconnected form of collaboration – one that i'm very keen on for reasons i'm not exactly sure about – but which i think would be great to think about for the conclusion of this book. am i getting too abstract?